ISO 9001:2000
Management
Responsibility
In a Nutshell

A Concise Guide

for Management

ISO 9001:2000 Management Responsibility In a Nutshell

A Concise Guide
for Management

Jeanne Ketola & Kathy Roberts

Paton
Press

Chico, California

Most Paton Press books are available at quantity discounts when purchased in bulk. For more information, contact:

Paton Press
P.O. Box 44
Chico, CA 95927-0044
Telephone: (530) 342-5480
Fax: (530) 342-5471
E-mail: *books@patonpress.com*
Web: *www.patonpress.com*

04 03 02 01   5 4 3 2 1

ISBN 0-9650445-8-0

Staff
Publisher .... Scott M. Paton
Senior Editor .... Vanessa R. Franco
Assistant Editor .... Heidi M. Paton
Book Cover Design .... Edward C. Jones

Dedication

To Mom and Dad, who always said I could;
Chuck, Tim, Lida, and Jon, who inspire me every day;
My clients, who challenge themselves to be the best.

—Jeanne

To Ryan, who is my soulmate and best friend,
and to Austin, who is my pride and joy.
Thanks for reminding me what's important in life.

—Kathy

Contents

Chapter 1

Introduction

After the publication of *ISO 9000:2000 In a Nutshell* in March 2000, we were frequently asked how ISO 9001:2000 would affect the role of management responsibility in the quality management system. Most of the people we talked to either were managers or were concerned about their organization's management team. Specifically, they wanted to know what managers would need to do to meet ISO 9001:2000's new requirements.

This book is a direct result of this need and is written specifically for management, including executive management, middle management, ISO coordinators, and management representatives. It is written in the same style as our first book, *ISO 9000:2000 In a Nutshell,* and designed to give managers a concise guide to everything they need to know about the changes to management's role in order to meet the ISO 9001:2000 requirements.

This book focuses on management responsibility, management commitment, quality planning and objectives, management review, management representatives, customers, and continual improvement.

Without a doubt, top management will be required to actively participate in the organization's quality management system by developing and implementing quality objectives and periodically evaluating the health of the system. They will also need to clearly understand what their customers' requirements are and ensure that those requirements result in an acceptable product and/or service. Furthermore, top management will need to ensure that the effectiveness of the system is continually improved.

Many managers we have talked with about these requirements approve of top management's added responsibility to support and guide the system. Many feel that without top management commitment, the energy and time spent maintaining the system is wasted. Many are convinced that without top management support, improvements will be minimal or non-existent.

In a nutshell, making improvement and gaining value from a quality management system is in the hands of top management. They must recognize that the effectiveness of the quality management system is their responsibility and no longer falls solely on the shoulders of the quality manager and/or ISO coordinator. We wish all managers great success in implementing ISO 9001:2000's new requirements and hope that this book makes their journey a little smoother.

Introduction In a Nutshell...

● Top management must actively participate in the organization's quality management system by developing and implementing quality objectives and periodically evaluating the health of the system.

● Top management must clearly understand customer requirements and ensure those requirements result in an acceptable product and/or service.

● Top management must ensure that the effectiveness of the quality management system is continually improved.

"Without top management commitment, the energy and time spent maintaining the system is wasted."

Chapter 2

Management Responsibility Overview

T he 1994 version of the ISO 9000 series of standards contained very basic requirements for management. Management's primary responsibility was to establish a quality policy and quality objectives and communicate these to the rest of the organization. In some organizations, this meant that the responsibility for the quality management system was addressed through an organizational chart, the torch was passed to a management representative to set up the documentation, and key members of management sat through a long meeting one to four times a year to review the quality "system."

One of the key criticisms of the 1994 version has been that management's role was minimal and that the requirements did not push management to move beyond maintenance and into the improvement arena. In fact, many viewed the 1994 standards as a "foundation" only and did not consider them a vehicle to propel a company to world-class status.

Management responsibility takes on a new dimension in ISO 9001:2000. The revised standard shifts the responsibility of the quality management system from the quality assurance department to top management, ensuring that:

■ Customer requirements are determined and met with the aim of enhancing customer satisfaction

■ Planning activities include quality objectives at each relevant function and level within the organization

■ Internal communication processes are established

■ Evidence is provided of management's commitment to develop and implement the quality management system and continually improve its effectiveness

■ Management review meeting activities include evaluating the quality management system's effectiveness, determining improvement opportunities, and identifying the need for changes to the quality management system

FOUNDATION OF ISO 9001:2000

Eight quality management principles form the foundation on which ISO 9001:2000 was developed. These principles are found in *ISO 9000:2000 Quality management systems—Fundamentals and vocabulary* and *ISO 9004:2000 Quality management systems—Guidelines for performance improvements*. They focus on business excellence and emphasize customer satisfaction. A quality management principle is a fundamental belief focused on continual performance improvement, attained by addressing the needs of customers and stakeholders. The principles are as follows:

1. *Customer Focus*—Organizations consider customers' current and future needs, meet customer requirements, and strive to exceed customer expectations.
2. *Leadership*—Leaders establish the organization's purpose and direction and create an environment in which people can be involved in achieving organizational objectives.
3. *Involvement of People*—An organization's people are its essence and their involvement and abilities enable the organization to benefit.
4. *Process Approach*—A process approach to managing resources and activities will more efficiently produce the desired results.
5. *System Approach to Management*—An organization's efficiency and effectiveness can be improved by identifying, understanding, and managing a system of interrelated processes.
6. *Continual Improvement*—An organization should have continual improvement as a permanent objective.
7. *Factual Approach to Decision Making*—Organizations should analyze data and information to make effective decisions.
8. *Mutually Beneficial Supplier Relationships*—Both the organization and its suppliers can create value by developing mutually beneficial, interdependent relationships.

For each of these principles, top management should evaluate the organization and determine the level at which the organization currently operates. Once this is done, top management can determine the actions necessary to close the gaps between current reality and the desired future state. Understanding these principles and how they apply will be critical in moving the organization toward business excellence.

A QUICK GLANCE AT MANAGEMENT'S ROLE

The requirements for management have been greatly enhanced in ISO 9001:2000. Section 5 Management responsibility focuses on management's role in leading the organization. Several components exist within this framework, such as determining the quality policy and quality objectives; demonstrating management commitment; and evaluating, maintaining, and continually improving the performance of the quality management system. The following summary provides a high-level view of management's responsibility:

1. Top management is responsible for establishing the quality policy and ensuring that it is communicated within the organization. The quality policy has to demonstrate management's commitment to meeting requirements and to continual improvement of the quality management system's effectiveness. ISO 9001:2000 requires that there be consistency between the quality policy and the quality objectives.

2. ISO 9001:2000 does not require as many documented procedures, allowing organizations to become more flexible in defining the amount of documentation needed by the organization. However, this does not mean the organization can pitch its current documentation. The standard specifically states that the organization will be required to identify the processes needed for the quality management system and the documentation necessary to ensure effective planning, operation, and control of the processes. With this more flexible approach, top management will need to be clear in determining and communicating responsibilities and authorities in order for the processes to be linked and clearly understood.

3. Top management has the ultimate responsibility for ensuring that adequate resources are provided throughout the organization to implement and continually improve the effectiveness of the quality management system. The organization must ensure that personnel are competent, based on their education, training, skills, and experience. Furthermore, the organization must determine and provide resources to implement, maintain, and improve the quality management system, as appropriate. Top management must also determine resources specific to product and for enhancing customer satisfaction.

4. The management representative now has the additional responsibility of ensuring the promotion of the awareness of customer requirements throughout the organization.

5. Top management is required to ensure that quality management system planning is performed. Planning must meet quality objectives and achieve the requirements described in Section 4.1 General, which include:

■ Identifying processes needed for the quality management system and their application

■ Determining the sequence and interaction of these processes

■ Determining criteria and methods for the effective operation and control of these processes
■ Ensuring availability of resources and information to support the operation and monitoring of the processes
■ Monitoring, measuring, and analyzing the processes
■ Implementing actions necessary to achieve planned results and continual improvement of these processes
■ Controlling of outsourced processes

6. The purpose of the management review process is to periodically evaluate the performance of the quality management system for suitability, adequacy, and effectiveness. The main intent of these reviews is to determine the health of the quality management system by identifying opportunities for improvement and determining actions to facilitate the improvement. ISO 9001:2000 specifies inputs and outputs to the management review process, including the evaluation of changes that could affect the quality management system. Furthermore, it directly links the management review process to the continual improvement of the organization.

DETAILS OF SECTION 5 MANAGEMENT RESPONSIBILITY

To help sort through the revision and determine the changes to management responsibility, the following summary has been provided. The *What's Clarified* section describes requirements that were present in the 1994 version but which have been clarified and more explicitly stated in the 2000 revision. The *What's New* section describes those requirements that are not present in the 1994 version but are included in the 2000 revision. The *What's the Same* section describes the requirements that are in both the 1994 version and the 2000 revision. The last section, *What's Not Included,* lists the requirements from 1994 that are not included in the 2000 revision.

WHAT'S CLARIFIED

■ Top management, specifically, must establish the organization's quality policy and ensure that the quality objectives are established at relevant functions and levels in the organization. The management review should be used to evaluate the need for changes to the quality management system, quality policy, and quality objectives. *(Reference 5.1 Management commitment; 5.4.1 Quality objectives; 5.6.1 General)*

■ The quality policy must be communicated and understood within the organization rather than implemented and maintained at all levels. *(Reference 5.3 Quality policy)*

■ Top management has the responsibility for, and must provide evidence of, their commitment to ensure the availability of resources and information. *(Reference 4.1 General requirements; 5.1 Management commitment)*

■ Top management must ensure that responsibilities and authorities are defined. This must be communicated within the organization. *(Reference 5.5.1 Responsibility and authority)*

■ Organizations must determine quality objectives and requirements that are specific to the product as appropriate. *(Reference 7.1 Planning of product realization)*

WHAT'S NEW

■ Top management must provide evidence of their commitment to system development, implementation and continual improvement of its effectiveness, which includes communicating to the organization the importance of meeting customer, regulatory, and statutory requirements. *(Reference 5.1 Management commitment)*

■ Top management must ensure that customer requirements are determined and met with the aim of enhancing customer satisfaction. *(Reference 5.2 Customer focus)*

■ Top management must ensure that the quality policy:
- Includes a commitment to meeting requirements and continual improvement of the effectiveness of the quality management system
- Provides a framework for quality objectives
- Is reviewed for ongoing suitability

(Reference 5.3 Quality policy)

■ Quality objectives must be established at relevant functions and levels. They must be measurable and consistent with the quality policy. Objectives must include those needed to meet product requirements. *(Reference 5.4.1 Quality objectives; 7.1 Planning of product realization)*

■ Planning must be performed to meet quality objectives and requirements in section 4.1 General. *(Reference 5.4.2 Quality management system planning)*

■ The integrity of the quality management system must be maintained when changes are planned or made to the system. *(Reference 5.4.2 Quality management system planning)*

■ The management representative has the authority and responsibility to promote the awareness of customer requirements throughout the organization. *(Reference 5.5.2 Management representative)*

■ Top management must ensure that processes for internal communication are established and that the communication takes place within the organization regarding the effectiveness of the quality management system and related processes. *(Reference 5.5.3 Internal communication)*

■ Management reviews must cover specific inputs and outputs during the review. The management review must also include assessing opportunities for improvement and evaluating any changes that could affect the quality management system, including the quality policy and quality objectives. *(Reference 5.6 Management review)*

■ Inputs to the management review must include:
  • Audit results
  • Feedback from customers
  • Analyses of process performance and product conformance
  • Preventive and corrective actions status
  • Follow-up actions from previous management reviews
  • Any changes that might affect the quality management system
  • Improvement recommendations
  (Reference 5.6.2 Review input)

■ Outputs of the management review must include decisions and actions relating to:
  • The quality management system (and its processes) improvement
  • Product improvement (related to customer requirements)
  • Resource needs
  (Reference 5.6.3 Review output)

■ Organizations must determine and provide the resources necessary to implement, maintain, and improve the effectiveness of the quality management system and to enhance customer satisfaction. *(Reference 6.1 Provision of resources)*

■ Organizations must ensure that personnel who perform work that affects product quality are competent, as well as determine what defines this competence. *(Reference 6.2.1 General; 6.2.2 Competence, awareness, and training)*

■ The organization must plan and implement the monitoring, measurement, analysis, and continual improvement processes to ensure confor-

mity of product, conformity of the quality management system, and achieve improvement of the quality management system. *(Reference 8.1 General).*
■ Requirements for attaining improvement are more specific. Organizations must continually improve the effectiveness of the quality management system through the use of the quality policy, quality objectives, audit results, data analysis, corrective/preventive actions, and management review. *(Reference 8.5.1 Continual improvement)*

WHAT'S THE SAME

■ Organizations must establish and document a quality policy and quality objectives and their commitment to them.
■ The quality policy must be relevant to organizational goals and customer requirements.
■ The quality policy must be disseminated throughout the organization.
■ Responsibilities and authorities must be defined and communicated.
■ Top management must allocate adequate resources to the quality management system.
■ The management representative must be a member of management who has defined responsibility and authority on matters relating to the quality system.
■ Top management is responsible for periodic quality system review to ensure its suitability and effectiveness.
■ Management review records must be kept.

WHAT'S NOT INCLUDED

■ The specific list of actions for personnel who affect quality
■ Responsibility and authority for personnel who affect quality
■ Specific language regarding types of resources (i.e., trained personnel) for management, for performance of work, and for verification activities, including audits

IN A NUTSHELL

Gone are the days when only the management representative was responsible for all facets of the quality management system. Now, ISO 9001:2000 explicitly directs top management to expand their role. Management will need to actively participate in reviewing the quality management system performance and identifying improvement opportunities relating to changing circumstances within the organization, process and product conformance analysis, and customer feedback, just to name a few. While the standard applies to the organization as a whole, many of the requirements will need top management's specific involvement in determining the methods and policies surrounding these requirements. Furthermore, top management's direction and leadership will be necessary to meet the intent of ISO 9001:2000's requirements.

Management Responsibility In a Nutshell...

● The revised standard shifts the responsibility of the quality management system from the quality assurance department to top management.

● Eight quality management principles form the foundation on which ISO 9001:2000 was developed.

● Top management is responsible for establishing the quality policy and ensuring that it is communicated within the organization.

● Top management has the ultimate responsibility for ensuring that adequate resources are provided throughout the organization to implement and continually improve the effectiveness of the quality management system.

"ISO 9001:2000
explicitly directs
top management to
expand their role."

Chapter 3

Management Commitment

here's an old saying, "The chicken is involved, but the pig is committed." In other words, the pig puts its heart and soul (and a few more body parts) into the process. The same analogy can be applied to organizations. When asking managers if they are committed to their organizations, who would say "no"? However, when asked to demonstrate that commitment, how many can do this with ease?

Many organizations struggle when top management's actions don't match their words. This lack of commitment leads to frustrated employees who are left to determine whether they work for an organization that is committed to providing its customers with a superior product and/or service as well as providing them with an acceptable work environment. Organizations often attempt to display their commitment to quality through slogans, banners, wallet cards, employee lunches, and the like. Although these things may help spread the quality message, commitment to quality is most effectively demonstrated when top management models commitment through actions. It's not uncommon to hear managers supporting their quality management system, but their actions often circumvent the system. (An example would be managers allowing the shipment of suspect product even though organizational quality procedures forbid shipping potentially nonconforming product to the customer.) Sometimes this happens when the month-end numbers from accounting to top management aren't as good as was expected. Therefore, quantity is more important than quality. This sends a mixed message that the managers may be committed but don't need to follow the rules.

During the push for total quality management in the 1980s, management commitment was discussed, but many didn't understand its essence. Committing to uphold a quality system is similar to committing to lose 10 pounds or quit smoking: It usually requires rethinking one's approach and then taking action. Commitment doesn't happen unless there is passion for the change or the goal. How many organizations have decided to become ISO 9001-registered because they have the passion, energy, and enthusiasm to believe that ISO 9001 is a great tool for improvement? What results do they show vs. the organizations that seek ISO 9001 registration because they have to or to win another corporate trophy? Many managers support ISO 9001 initially, but, just like a diet, decide that following the necessary rules every day is too much work. They try to outmaneuver the system by agreeing ISO 9001 is a good thing but then disregard the requirements. For commitment to be demonstrable, the passion must be there and a transformation must take place in management's thinking. This transformation moves the organization past the belief that ISO 9001 is merely a bunch of documents to the idea that ISO 9001 is a tool that can help improve the organization. It also signifies that this is a way the organization does business and that everyone is responsible for following the system. Furthermore, those organizations that are successfully moving beyond ISO 9001 continuously look for ways to improve the system. To demonstrate true commitment, management should not exempt anyone from the requirements of the system—including themselves.

Although management commitment was implied in the standard's 1994 version, ISO 9001:2000 includes a broader requirement under Section 5.1 Management commitment. This section states that top management must provide evidence of its commitment to the development, implementation, and continual improvement of the quality management system's effectiveness by:

(a) Communicating to the organization the importance of meeting customer as well as statutory and regulatory requirements

(b) Establishing the quality policy

(c) Ensuring that quality objectives are established

(d) Conducting management reviews

(e) Ensuring the availability of resources

Top management should treat these requirements seriously and offer tangible evidence that this is the case. By weaving the requirements into the existing operation and making them a part of the organization's overall philosophy, the organization can start to move beyond the belief that ISO 9001 is a set of rules separate from normal operations. This deliberate approach will also help demonstrate to the organization that top management is committed to the integrity of the quality management system and that they have taken the time to understand and incorporate these concepts into the overall organizational framework.

SECTION 5.1 MANAGEMENT COMMITMENT

The following paragraphs describe the intent of each 5.1 subsection and include tips for implementation.

Top management must demonstrate commitment to the development and improvement of the quality management system by confirmation of the following:

(a) *Communicating to the organization the importance of meeting customer as well as statutory and regulatory requirements*

Intent: To ensure that top management effectively communicates why customer, legal, and regulatory requirements are important to the organization

TIPS FOR IMPLEMENTATION

■ Develop a plan for communication. This should include frequency, the methods that will be used, and those who will be involved in assisting with the communications. For example, top management may educate their direct reports on the importance of the customer, legal, and regulatory requirements. Each level would subsequently educate the next level. This plan would become part of addressing the requirements in 5.5.3 Internal communication.

■ Implement supporting methods of communication, such as the company newsletter, intranet/e-mail messages, screen-saver messages, bulletin boards, companywide meetings, or other methods appropriate for the organization's size. Posting information such as compliance regulations, customer requirements, and relevant correspondence may also be helpful. To maintain consistency of the communications, it's beneficial to document the methods, frequency, and responsibility for the communications when implementing the overall process.

(b) *Establishing the quality policy*
(c) *Ensuring quality objectives are established*

Intent: To ensure that top management establishes an organizational quality policy and determines quality objectives consistent with the policy.

■ Review the organizational quality policy and determine if any changes are needed. Determine if the intent of the policy is affected by changing business conditions and ensure that the policy is documented.

■ Ensure that all company personnel understand the quality policy and can restate it in their own words. It's not necessary for employees to memorize the quality policy, but they should be able to explain how they are able to achieve the intent of the policy in their day-to-day activities.

■ Determine and document organizational quality objectives. Ensure that they are reviewed periodically and changed as needed. The quality objectives must be measurable and addressed during management review meetings.

■ Ensure that the objectives align with the policy and that employees understand how the policy and objectives relate to their work. Post this information in a way that demonstrates to employees how they contribute to achieving these objectives.

See Chapter 5, Quality Policies, Planning, and Objectives for more information.

(d) *Conducting management reviews*

Intent: To ensure that top management periodically evaluates the effectiveness of the organization's quality management system, assesses opportunities for improvement, and determines the need for changes to the quality management system.

■ Define an appropriate management review cycle for the organization (e.g., annually, semiannually, quarterly). This cycle should be defined in the quality management system.

■ Ensure that the appropriate management personnel actively participate in the review process by attending meetings and providing the requested information. At a minimum, this should include the most senior members of management, as defined by the quality management system and the management representative.

■ Clearly document the minutes of the management review meetings and distribute them to designated personnel. Minutes should accurately capture the discussions, decisions, and actions to be taken.

■ Determine the retention time for management review records. Management review records are regularly reviewed by third-party auditors and should be kept at least three years to allow for a three-year review.

■ Ensure that all improvement opportunities relating to audit results, customer feedback, product conformance, process performance, status of corrective/preventive actions, previous management review actions, resources, and potential changes to the quality management system have been reviewed. This can be accomplished by gathering data and using graphs and charts to review trends.

■ As a result of this review, establish specific actions for the improvement of the effectiveness of the quality management system and assign ownership.

■ Ensure follow-up on all actions that are established, documented, and assigned from the management review meetings. Record the results of the actions taken.

See Chapter 6, Management Review, for more information.

(e) *Ensuring the availability of resources*

Intent: To ensure that top management provides necessary resources for the development, implementation, maintenance, and continual improvement of the effectiveness of the organization's quality management system

TIPS FOR IMPLEMENTATION

■ Ensure that all quality planning and/or management review documentation includes the assignment of adequate resources for quality activities. This includes the allocation of resources to carry out internal audits, preventive maintenance, inspections, training, and so on.

■ Develop an organizational chart that shows the assignment of responsibilities. This chart should be considered a living document and may require modifications when there are changes to the quality management system.

EFFECTIVE ALLOCATION OF RESOURCES

Management's commitment to the allocation of adequate resources is an important requirement found throughout ISO 9001:2000. The following sections identify the specific need for resources:

■ *5.1 Management commitment.* Ensure the availability of resources.

■ *5.4.2 Quality management system planning.* Ensure that planning is carried out to meet 4.1 General requirements, which includes ensuring the availability of necessary resources and information to support the operation and monitoring of the processes.

■ *5.6 Management review.* Include decisions and actions taken related to resource needs.

■ *6.1 Provision of resources.* Determine and provide resources for implementing, maintaining and continually improving the effectiveness of the quality management system as well as enhancing customer satisfaction.

■ *7.1 Planning of product realization.* Provide resources specific to the product.

In any organization, the resources required to produce a system output include materials, information, environment, equipment, and people. The standard specifically requires top management to ensure resource availability. It also requires that resources be tied to the achievement of organizational objectives and that employees understand how they contribute to the achievement of these objectives.

10 POINTS FOR COMMITMENT

Top management can use the following 10 points as a barometer to measure their commitment to the organization's quality management system:

1. Time is allocated to communicate organizational objectives in such a way that employees understand their importance and know how they contribute to achieving these objectives.

2. Adequate resources are planned and provided for the quality management system. Enough time is allowed for people to meet and discuss issues that affect the quality management system. For example, internal audits are not canceled. Preventive maintenance activities are considered important and not disregarded. Training is not the first thing that gets cut.

3. Management actively participates in management review meetings and any other meetings where assistance is required for the guidance on the quality management system.

4. Important information about the customer is known and actively discussed within the organization.

5. Management participates, as appropriate, in resolving customer issues.

6. Employee involvement is encouraged on matters relating to the quality management system. Comments and suggestions for improvements are welcomed from all levels in the organization.

7. Other managers' decisions about improvements to the quality management system are welcomed. This may include allocating time, money, and people.

8. Relevant and timely information is consistently communicated so that everyone is aware of the ups and downs of the organization.

9. Personnel are encouraged to take risks and solve problems and are rewarded for being proactive.

10. Actions clearly demonstrate that management "walks the talk." Employees can see, hear, and feel this commitment and, therefore, don't discuss the lack of it during lunchroom conversations.

IN A NUTSHELL

Although ISO 9001:2000 specifically requires top management commitment, it should be noted that all levels of management need to demonstrate their commitment. This means that if top management is doing their part, middle management must also support and commit to the changes. Far too often, middle management becomes the stumbling block to change, because they agree with top management in management meetings but return to their departments to criticize the changes, leaving the rest of the personnel confused about the organization's commitment to quality.

To successfully meet this requirement, top management should take a serious look at how they define "commitment" within the management team. Through the successful demonstration of this commitment, managers will provide the workforce with a clear vision of what's important to the organization and where it is headed. In return, the workforce will provide management with their commitment to providing superior products and/or services to their stakeholders.

Management Commitment In a Nutshell...

● Commitment to quality is most effectively demonstrated when top management models commitment through actions.

● Top management must provide evidence of its commitment to the development, implementation, and continual improvement of the quality management system's effectiveness.

● By weaving the requirements into the existing operation and making them a part of the organization's overall philosophy, the organization can start to move beyond the belief that ISO 9001 is a set of rules separate from normal operations.

● The resources required to produce a system output include materials, information, environment, equipment, and people.

"For commitment to be demonstrable, the passion must be there and a transformation must take place in management's thinking."

Chapter 4

Management Representative

The ISO 9001:2000 standard requires top management to appoint a management member who has the responsibility and authority to:

■ Ensure that the processes of the quality management system are established, implemented, and maintained

■ Report to top management on the performance of the quality management system, including any improvement needs

■ Ensure that the awareness of customer requirements throughout the organization is promoted

SELECTING THE MANAGEMENT REPRESENTATIVE

Selecting the right person to coordinate and facilitate the implementation and maintenance of the quality management system is a critical task. This person must be someone who has the necessary skills and is respected by people within the company. It also means that top management must actively support the management representative's actions and keep the lines of communication open.

Many quality management systems go astray from the beginning because management appoints someone they don't really support. Top management should view the management representative as a partner who can help facilitate change. Without this solid relationship, implementing, maintaining, or improving the quality management system will become an exercise in frustration.

When selecting a management representative, management should consider candidates with the following attributes:

■ Knowledge of the organization, including its politics

■ Enough authority to implement change or improvements

■ Strong enough to withstand the pressure from the potential opposition to ISO 9001

- Organizational skills
- Leadership skills
- Self-motivation
- Perceived as a liaison to top management
- Trusted by top management
- Trusted by all personnel
- Good communicator
- Risk taker
- Understands the components of a quality management system
- Understands the concept of linking systems and processes
- Knowledgeable about ISO 9001:2000
- Understands the organization's quality policy and quality objectives

Management representatives should be included in management and planning meetings that involve the quality management system because they can often make recommendations on how to handle the impact of change on multiple departments. Moreover, because management representatives typically have intimate knowledge of the quality management system, they are able to provide timely, valuable feedback during the planning activities.

In contrast, management representatives who are excluded from these activities aren't as effective, nor can they help the organization stay compliant with the system when organizational changes are on the horizon. Keep in mind that ISO 9001:2000 requires top management to review changes that may affect the quality management system and to ensure the integrity of the system is maintained when changes are planned and implemented.

Management representatives need top management's support and backing. That's why it's important that management select someone they respect and with whom they're comfortable working. Often, management themselves sabotage the management representative. For example, the first time another manager or employee complains about changes, the management representative takes the blame. This might make the representative less likely to take risks and more inclined to dance around his or her colleagues when trying to implement change, thus creating a less effective management system.

Good management representatives are worth their weight in gold. However, far too many burn out fighting for change in a thankless position. If top management is serious about developing an effective quality management system, they need to allow the management representative to do the job and reward him or her for the improvements achieved. They also need to evaluate the amount of resources it takes to manage the quality management system. Many management representatives wear so many hats that they aren't effective in any of the jobs they perform, much less successful at facilitating improvements that could have financial significance for the company.

WHAT TO EXPECT FROM A MANAGEMENT REPRESENTATIVE

How much a person can handle in this position is relative to the size of the organization. In small to mid-size companies, management representatives will often handle more activities associated with the quality management system than will those in larger companies. However, top management must decide how much time their management representative can devote to different activities and still be effective. This decision should be made with the management representative, who has working knowledge of how many hours are required to do the job. In some organizations, management representatives have been known to handle the document control system, coordinate internal audits, lead the corrective action and customer complaint systems, coordinate plant tours, direct management reviews, and handle the responsibilities of a full-time position in addition to their management representative responsibilities. These people routinely put in 60 to 70 hours a week trying to keep the system in place. Even though people today are required to wear many hats in most organizations, it's unreasonable to expect an individual to handle this type of schedule and responsibility and still be effective.

If the management representative is trying to do it all, there is a good chance that the improvements aren't going to happen. Taking on too many responsibilities doesn't leave much time to investigate problems or facilitate problem-solving teams. Also, by having management representatives handle so much of the quality management system by themselves, a distorted message is sent to the rest of the organization that ISO 9001 isn't part of the company's operations. Furthermore, if management representatives are doing it all, the entire system is jeopardized if they leave the organization.

RULE OF THUMB

If the quality management system is just getting started, the management representative will need to devote most of his or her time to establishing and implementing the system. This would be a good time for the management representative to clear his or her agenda and focus on this important function without the interruption of other activities.

Once a system has been established and the organization has a few external audits under its belt, the management representative can focus on analysis of data generated by the quality management system and refining problem-solving activities. The management representative should start to look at the cost savings associated with improvements that have either been implemented or will be implemented. The management representative can also play a major role in assisting top management with prioritizing improvement activities resulting from management reviews. Once the system is established, and depending on the size of the organization, the management representative may be able to take on other responsibilities while focusing primarily on the organization's improvement activities.

Spreading out the wealth of activity also helps to educate and include others in the responsibility of the system. For instance, resources needed to assist a management representative for a typical quality management system for a 350- to 400-person company may include those listed below. These positions may be full- or part-time depending on the nature of the business.

■ Assistant to the management representative
■ Document control coordinator
■ Audit support or audit coordinator

Another area that warrants more participation from others is management review. It's not uncommon to see management representatives trying to pull all of the information together for the review, schedule and conduct the meetings, and take notes. Information analysis for management reviews should be delegated to those responsible for managing the activity. For example, a management representative may delegate the analysis of information as shown in Table 4.1.

Table 4.1 presents an efficient way to organize the information, responsibility, and frequency of collection. The frequency of collection describes the time frame in which the information should be compiled in preparation for management review.

Leading the meetings is also an important task, and top management should take this opportunity to demonstrate and model their leadership skills to the rest of the team. See Chapter 6, Management Review, for more information.

Table 4.1: Data Collection for Management Review

Trended Information	Responsibility	Frequency of Collection
Audit Results	Management Representative/ Quality Manager	Biannual
Customer Feedback	Sales/Customer/ Marketing Manager	Quarterly
Corrective/Preventive Action Status	Management Representative/ Quality Manager	Quarterly
Nonconforming Reports	Production Manager	Monthly
Supplier Performance	Purchasing Manager	Quarterly
Quality Policy and Quality Objectives	Top Management	Yearly

ASSIGNING MORE THAN ONE MANAGEMENT REPRESENTATIVE

Top management may appoint more than one management representative. This is a management decision and should be determined by the organization's needs. In larger, multisite organizations, it's not uncommon for a corporate management representative and site-specific management representatives to be appointed. Appointing two people to share the same position at one facility may also be an option.

Communication must be at its optimum for the concept of multiple representatives to be successful. If two people are sharing the same job within the same facility, they must have a strategy in place for working together. This should include clearly identified responsibilities, division of workload and scheduled feedback meetings. Furthermore, they must be familiar with the quality policy and objectives of the organization so they can support management. Consequently, top management will now have two instead of one person to work with. Because of this added dimension, top management should ensure that the representatives hear a consistent message and receive the same direction.

If the organization is multisite with a corporate management representative and site-specific representatives, it's typically the responsibility of the corporate representative to ensure that consistency prevails between the corporate and the individual sites. Again, this approach requires planning and good communication. If the corporate site is involved in portions of the individual site's system (i.e., evaluation of suppliers, maintenance of records associated with the system, supplying internal auditors), then the quality management system documentation will need to explain how the responsibilities and systems are linked. It should be clear where the responsibility of one facility stops and the other begins.

IN A NUTSHELL

Management representatives play an important role in ensuring that the quality management system is established, implemented, and maintained. They also are responsible for reporting to top management on the quality management system's performance and any need for improvement. However, the management representatives should not be held responsible to run the entire quality management system by themselves. They need top management's support and guidance. By having the management representatives and top management work together, the benefits are greater and the improvement activities stay in the forefront of the organization's game plan.

Management Representative In a Nutshell...

● Selecting the right person to coordinate and facilitate the implementation and maintenance of the quality management system is critical.

● Management representatives should be included in management and planning meetings that involve the quality management system.

● Management representatives need top management's support and backing.

● Top management may appoint more than one management representative.

"Top management should view the management representative as a partner who can facilitate change."

Chapter 5

Quality Policies, Planning, and Objectives

T he 1994 versions of the ISO 9000 standards contained a rather confusing paragraph about quality planning. Auditors, consultants, and organizations had a difficult time determining if the standard was requiring them to carry out planning activities or to develop quality plans for production activities. The clause also contained a summary of some of the standard's requirements, which often prompted the questions: "Does this need to be addressed?" and "Aren't these things being done by setting up the quality system?"

ISO 9001:2000 eliminates this confusion because the standard is clearer about the organization's planning requirements. The requirements for the policy, objectives, and planning are found or linked to the following sections of ISO 9001:2000:

- 4.1 General requirements
- 5.1 Management commitment
- 5.3 Quality policy
- 5.4.1 Quality objectives
- 5.4.2 Quality management system planning
- 5.6 Management review
- 7.1 Planning of product realization
- 8.1 General
- 8.5.1 Continual improvement

Reviewing these requirements will present a good opportunity for top management to consider how their ISO 9001 efforts align with their overall organizational plans and allow them to move beyond the notion that an ISO 9001 quality management system is separate from the organization's business management system. The organization should scrutinize its quality policy and quality objectives to ensure that both are in sync. For example, does the quality policy refer to satisfying the customer but fail to define specific objectives for achieving customer satisfaction?

Remember that these requirements are the responsibility of top management, who have been defined by *ISO 9000:2000 Quality management systems—Fundamentals and vocabulary* as the person or group of people who direct and control an organization at the highest level.

THE QUALITY POLICY

Top management may wonder if the work they are doing in formulating mission statements is separate from or the same as the quality policy. *ISO 9000:2000 Quality management systems—Fundamentals and vocabulary* defines a quality policy as a statement that: "Defines the overall intentions and direction of an organization related to quality as formally expressed by top management." ISO 9001:2000 requires that the quality policy is consistent with and provides a framework for quality objectives.

A mission statement is commonly defined as a statement that communicates reason for existing by describing the organization's purpose, reflecting key customer needs and creating the backbone for planning and goal setting.

The definitions are very similar. Some organizations have incorporated their quality policy into their mission statements, whereas others have elected to have both a mission statement and a quality policy. The choice is up to the organization. However, whatever is decided, the statement(s) should reflect the intention and direction of the organization and should coincide with and be reflective of the objectives or goals. Management should ask themselves seriously if they have clearly defined the purpose of their business and if stakeholders would concur. Often, mission statements or quality policies do a poor job of defining what the organization is in business to do. Organizations shouldn't copy or mimic other organizations' quality policies or mission statements due to the differences between businesses. This is why it's important for top management to take the time to define and polish this statement, as they have the key information that can link the purpose of the organization to its performance. To help top management assess or revisit their quality policy/mission statement, ISO 9001:2000's quality policy requirements have been broken down as follows:

ISO 9001:2000 requires top management to establish the quality policy to ensure that it:

1. *Is appropriate for the purpose of the organization.* Top management

must establish the policy and ensure that it adequately defines the purpose of the organization. Management should ask: Does our policy clearly state the prime focus of the business? And is this statement clear enough to set the stage for establishing objectives? All members of top management should participate in developing this policy.

2. *Includes a commitment to comply with requirements and continually improve the effectiveness of the quality management system.* The policy itself should state management's commitment to ensure that the product or service requirements that satisfy the customer are met and that the organization is working toward continual improvement.

3. *Provides a framework for establishing and reviewing quality objectives.* Management must ensure that the concepts outlined in the policy are supported by measurable objectives. These objectives form the foundation of the continual improvement effort. Without them, organizations will continue to operate like rudderless ships. Furthermore, these objectives should be relevant to personnel so they understand how they personally contribute to attaining the objectives.

4. *Is communicated and understood within the organization.* Management must ensure that they have developed a method for communicating the policy. This may be in the form of posted policies, wallet cards, screen savers, or other methods that convey the message. These methods should ensure that personnel have a clear understanding of what the quality policy and objectives mean to them in their day-to-day activities and how they achieve the objectives. It's advisable to include personnel from various departments when determining the plans for achieving objectives. This helps individuals understand how they contribute to the overall success of the organization.

5. *Is reviewed for continuing suitability.* The policy must be reviewed and revised, if necessary, to ensure that it continues to fit the organization. This review is required during management review and will need to be documented. This review is important because organizations may find that policies need to be modified due to changing business conditions, such as expansion of product offerings, mergers, or acquisitions.

An example of a quality policy or mission statement is:

> *The EB Company provides Web page development products and services to organizations. We are committed to excellence in meeting our customers' requirements, maintaining employee satisfaction, and continually improving*

as a world-class company through partnerships with our suppliers.

THE QUALITY OBJECTIVES

In the 1994 versions of the standards, the requirements for quality objectives were blended into the requirements for the quality policy. The standard only specified that the objectives be documented. In fact, the requirements for the objectives seemed so insignificant that some third-party auditors didn't even check to see if objectives existed.

ISO 9000:2000 defines quality objectives as something sought or aimed for, related to quality. It also states that the objectives should generally be based on the quality policy and be specified at relevant functions and levels within the organization. ISO 9001:2000 requires that the organization spell out the goals that support its policy. Furthermore, these objectives or goals must be measurable and communicated within the organization so that personnel are aware of the relevance and importance of their activities and how they contribute to the achievement of these quality objectives. The quality objectives must also include those needed to meet the requirements for products. *(See 7.1 Planning of product realization)*

Because ISO 9001:2000 is founded on eight quality management principles, reviewing these principles may help management define their quality policy and develop their quality objectives. The eight principles below are also found in more detail in Chapter 2, Management Responsibility Overview, as well as in ISO 9000:2000.

The eight quality management principles are as follows:
1. Customer Focus
2. Leadership
3. Involvement of people
4. Process approach
5. System approach to management
6. Continual improvement
7. Factual approach to decision making
8. Mutually beneficial supplier relationships

An example of the relationship of the policy to the objectives is shown as follows according to the policy previously mentioned.

Quality Policy

> *The EB Company provides Web page development products and services to organizations. We are committed to excellence in meeting our customers' requirements, maintaining employee satisfaction, and continually improving as a world-class company through partnerships with our suppliers.*

The EB Company ensures its policy is carried out through the following objectives:

■ *Excellence with our Customers*: We establish and improve products, processes, and systems to ensure that our customer receives their products or services on time and as specified. We ensure that our pricing remains competitive in the marketplace.

■ *Excellence with Employees*: Through our leadership, we provide a climate conducive to personal development, equal opportunity, and participation for our employees. We do this by educating our workforce and providing the resources necessary for them to be able to serve the customer. We look to our employees for ways to improve our products, processes, and services.

■ *Excellence with our Suppliers*: We deal fairly and ensure mutual respect by partnering with our suppliers through open communication and full disclosure of our objectives.

Completing the policy and objectives is only part of the task. Management must also ensure that the objectives are broken down into strategies that can be assigned to relevant levels and functions and that resources needed to carry out the plans are available. This planning activity is the critical step in achieving continual improvement. Without detailed planning, there is a high risk that the policy and objectives will simply remain on paper or posted on a wall and never be converted into action.

QUALITY PLANNING

Top management must ensure that the planning of the quality management system is carried out to meet the following requirements:

■ Processes needed for the quality management system (taking into consideration any exclusions) and their application within the organization are identified.

■ Sequence and interaction of these processes are determined.

■ Operation and control of the processes are effective due to criteria and methods that have been decided upon.

■ Resources and information are made available to support the operation and monitoring of the processes.

■ Processes are monitored, measured, and analyzed.

■ Necessary actions are taken to achieve planned results and continual improvement of the processes.

■ Control of outsourced processes is ensured, when applicable.

Planning activities must be carried out to ensure that the quality objectives are met. This may show up in business planning minutes or documents, strategic plans, or other meetings where planning activities are done. Management must ensure that changes which could affect the quality management system, such as computerized systems, equipment changes, and personnel changes, are reviewed to maintain the integrity of the system.

A good source of information that can be incorporated into quality planning activities comes from management review meetings. Remember that the management review is a forum for looking at indicators or results from the quality management system. These results may not only be acted upon for improvement activities but may also provide management with information for carrying out planning activities. Furthermore, these results help determine resources such as human resource needs, equipment needs, and information.

LINKING THE QUALITY POLICY, QUALITY OBJECTIVES, AND PLANNING

The policy, objectives, and planning requirements of ISO 9001:2000 aren't meant to replace strategic planning within the organization but rather to work in conjunction with higher-level planning. If organizations are doing a good job of strategic planning, they most likely have gone through the analysis process of defining their business, defining key success factors, identifying their competitors' strengths and weaknesses, identifying market opportunities and threats, determining their competitive advantage, and determining potential strategies, which includes running a cost-benefit analysis on these strategies. It's important to mention that ISO 9001's customer, product, process, and continual improvement requirements should be taken into consideration when strategic planning events take place. Because the decisions made can have a profound impact on the quality management system, these considerations should not be left as a separate quality meeting run by the management representative. Also, if applicable, corporate-level mission statements and strategies should be incorporated as foundations for the required policy, objectives, and planning activities.

For smaller organizations with less formal strategic planning activities, the ISO 9001:2000 requirements for the linkage of policy, objectives, and basic planning will be a valuable addition to the overall performance of the organization.

EB COMPANY PLANNING CASE STUDY

The EB Company achieved ISO 9001 registration in 1992 and had worked diligently at applying the standard's requirements. Management had never conducted any formal strategic planning nor linked their policy, objectives, and planning activities together. However, through the management review process, management discovered problems with customer complaints, discount pricing, employee turnover, computer downtime, and supplier deliveries. After much discussion at the management level, they decided to revisit their planning process to better coordinate their objectives and planning so they could be more effective in implementing improvement activities. Because they had done a good job of presenting detailed analysis on the results of their system effectiveness during their management review meetings, it was easy to choose areas for improvement. The president facilitated the planning meetings that included all key members of the management staff. When managers developed the tactical plans, they included key individuals from their departments to participate in the planning process.

The result of their efforts is shown in the following tables, which demonstrate examples of their goals at both the strategic and tactical level in order to support their quality policy and objectives. While the EB Company's objectives are measurable, specific outcomes were also established for each tactical plan so that those responsible were certain of the expectations for completion. Even though more detail will be needed for the tactical plans, the matrixes provide a snapshot for management of the responsible parties, the status, the measurements, and the outcomes in order to achieve their goals.

Here's EB Company's quality policy again for reference:

> *The EB Company provides Web page development products and services to organizations. We are committed to excellence in meeting our customers' requirements, main-*

taining employee satisfaction, and continually improving as a world-class company through partnerships with our suppliers.

The EB Company ensures its policy is carried out through the following objectives:

OBJECTIVE 1: EXCELLENCE WITH CUSTOMERS

■ Establish and improve products, processes, and systems to ensure that our customers receive their products or services on time and as specified.
■ Ensure pricing remains competitive.

Based on their analysis, the following strategies were established to support their objectives:

Strategies— Objective 1	Person Responsible	Status	Measurements
1. Increase on-time deliveries from 92% to 97% by fourth quarter.	VP Operations	Open	On-time delivery
2. Decrease number of order entry errors from 25% to 5% by fourth quarter.	Customer Service Manager	Open	Order entry errors
3. Revise marketing plan and pricing strategy by second quarter.	VP Sales/ Marketing	Completed	Customer complaints regarding discount pricing

An example of a supporting tactical plan for strategy No. 3:

Tactical Plan for Strategy No. 3 (From Objective 1)	Person Responsible	Status	Outcomes
Hire customer survey company by second week of January. The focus of the survey is to determine competitor pricing strategy and to gather specific customer concerns related to pricing.	VP Sales/ Marketing	Completed	Survey company approved by top management and scheduled
Oversee completion of customer survey by the first week of March for incorporation into marketing plan.	VP Sales/ Marketing	Completed	Completed customer survey
Complete market research by first week of April.	VP Sales/ Marketing	Open	Completed market research report
Complete marketing plan and submit to planning team for approval by first week of May.	VP Sales/ Marketing	Open	Completed marketing plan
Based on market research, reissue pricing matrix to sales and marketing by first week of June.	VP Sales/ Sales Manager	Open	Revised pricing matrix implemented
Rewrite policy on authorization of discounts for new pricing by third week of June.	Sales Manager	Open	Revised policy on discounts submitted to management for approval

The EB Company has established measures to ensure the success of their objectives and to comply with ISO 9001:2000. Because the research and marketing plan helped to establish their pricing position, no further measurements will be needed. However, the EB Company is committed to reviewing their pricing structure on a yearly basis due to their fast-paced business climate. Because of the number of customer complaints due to confusion over their discount pricing strategy, they have established a measure for unauthorized discounts and will begin to measure the number of complaints regarding discounts after the policy is implemented in June.

OBJECTIVE 2: EXCELLENCE WITH EMPLOYEES

■ Provide personal development, equal opportunity, and participation for our employees as well as educate our workforce.

■ Provide the resources necessary for employees to be able to serve the customer.

■ Enable our employees to improve our products, processes, and services.

Strategies— Objective 2	Person Responsible	Status	Measurements
1. Decrease employee turnover from 35% to 20%.	VP of Human Resources	Open	Employee turn-over (Turnover reports)
2. Increase employee involvement on process improvement teams by 15%.	VP Manufac-turing and VP Sales and Marketing	Open	Percent involve-ment to number of employees. Also, track num-ber of employ-ees new to process teams vs. those who participated in the past.
3. Reduce computer down time due to over-loads by 25%.	MIS Director	Open	Unscheduled down time

Tactical Plans for Strategies No. 1, 2 & 3 (From Objective No. 2)	Person Responsible	Status	Outcomes
Identify training needs of managers and employees and submit budget by the end of the first quarter.	All Management	Completed	Identified training needs
Investigate need for employee incentive plan (e.g., profit sharing) by the end of the second quarter.	VP Human Resources	Open	Report submitted to top management outlining options
Establish a cross-functional process for improvement teams for critical product issues by end of first quarter.	VP Manufacturing and VP Sales and Marketing	Completed	Process established
Develop budget and implementation plan for new computer system modules for order entry and warehousing by end of second quarter.	President, Finance, Operations—managers from all departments affected by the change	Open	Prepared budget and implementation plan
Determine number of procedures and processes that will be affected by computer changes, including resources needed. Submit plan by end of second quarter for incorporation into computer implementation plan.	Management Representative	Open	Procedures determined and plan submitted

Objective 3: Excellence with our Suppliers

■ Ensure mutual respect by partnering with our suppliers through open communication and full disclosure of our objectives.

Strategies— Objective 3	Person Responsible	Status	Measurements
1. Reduce number of late deliveries by 15%.	Purchasing Director	Open	Monitor receiving reports and late shipment reports
2. Increase the number of preferred suppliers by 10%.	VP of Purchasing	Open	Number of preferred suppliers vs. total number of suppliers

Tactical Plans for Strategies No. 1 & 2 (From Objective 3)	Person Responsible	Status	Outcomes
Establish cross-functional supplier/management team and conduct first meeting to discuss late deliveries (include members from key suppliers) by second quarter.	Purchasing Manager/ Quality Manager	Open	Team established and first meeting recorded
Plan and conduct annual Supplier Day by end of the third quarter.	Purchasing Manager	Open	Event plan completed and documented, and Supplier Day held
Jointly develop key goals and measurements with suppliers by first quarter.	VP of Purchasing	Completed	Joint goals developed and documented

Breaking down the strategies for its objectives into tactical plans for the applicable departments helped the EB Company to comply with the standard, which requires that the objectives be established at relevant functions and levels. While ISO 9001:2000 doesn't specify how the plans should be documented, EB Company management felt they would be able to track their progress more efficiently if they used a formal method to document their strategies and action plans. The matrix provided a concise method to track the status of their plans during their monthly management meetings.

Summary of the EB Company's Planning Process

The EB Company established a correlation between their policy, objectives and planning activities as required by ISO 9001:2000. They included key individuals who would be affected by the plans in the planning sessions. This method helped create buy-in from the various departments and increased the likelihood that the plans would be successfully implemented. They met regularly to determine the status of the outcomes to ensure they were staying on track with the tactical plans. The EB Company also took into consideration the management representative's expertise when it was recognized that the changes they were planning would affect the quality management system. Because a cross section of people were involved in the planning, top management was able to communicate the plans effectively so employees knew how they would be involved in helping to achieve the objectives.

IN A NUTSHELL

Even though ISO 9001:2000 requires more from the user in terms of planning than did the 1994 version, the requirements are minimal compared to some of the more formal planning activities practiced by some organizations. Smaller to mid-size organizations often don't engage in formal or documented planning activities and may find these requirements challenging, but helpful, in beginning the planning process. It should be noted that many more facets to planning, such as market analysis, the identification of strengths and weaknesses, and determination of competitive advantages can be incorporated once an organization has become comfortable with the planning process and has met the minimum requirements of ISO 9001:2000.

Top management should consider the requirements of the quality management system and incorporate the policy and objectives into the bigger picture to avoid running the quality management system on a separate track. As with most things, less is better when establishing goals. Top management should not be overly zealous in assigning too many goals, which could result in the organization spending too much time trying to reorganize itself rather than service the customer. Top management should also take into consideration the magnitude of the goals. For example, operational changes, such as the implementation of new computer systems, will be more challenging than implementing a companywide training plan.

Finally, planning should include those who will be affected by the plans. The involvement of people who perform the tasks can provide needed insight for the implementation and communication of such plans. Management should also ensure that changes in the organization are fully communicated to the management representatives so that they help in identifying the changes that will be necessary to maintain the integrity of the quality management system.

As a final note, the development of objectives and strategic planning should not be confused with a financial business plan. Business plans are typically meant to sell investors on the idea of investing money. If an organization is only creating financial business plans (rather than strategic plans), it runs the risk of operating its business from a current financial picture instead of a strategic picture that positions it for the future.

Quality Policies, Planning, and Objectives In a Nutshell...

● The organization should scrutinize its quality policy and quality objectives to ensure that both are in sync.

● The quality policy should be consistent with and provide a framework for quality objectives.

● Planning activities must be carried out to ensure that the quality objectives are met.

● Objectives must be measurable and communicated within the organization so that personnel are aware of the relevance and importance of their activities and how they contribute to the achievement of these quality objectives.

"The policy, objectives, and planning requirements of ISO 9001:2000 aren't meant to replace strategic planning within the organization but rather to work in conjunction with higher-level planning."

Chapter 6

Management Review

ISO 9001:2000's requirements for management review may not have changed much for many in terms of the topics that are reviewed or how the meeting is conducted. However, the standard is now more specific about the content of the meetings and requires that the results of the reviews include decisions and actions surrounding improvement opportunities.

PURPOSE AND REQUIREMENTS OF MANAGEMENT REVIEW

The purpose of the management review process is for top management to periodically evaluate the suitability, adequacy, and the effectiveness of the quality management system. The main intent of these reviews is to determine the health of the quality management system by assessing opportunities for improvement and the need for changes to the quality management system, including the quality policy and quality objectives. If top management has delegated this review to others or infrequently attends, they aren't meeting the intent of the standard. ISO 9001:2000 specifies inputs and outputs to the management review process as follows:

Inputs
- Audit results
- Feedback from customers
- Process performance and product conformance
- Corrective/preventive action status
- Actions to be taken from previous management reviews
- Changes that may affect the quality management system
- Recommendations for improvement

Management must establish the frequency of the meetings and ensure that the results of the review are recorded. Furthermore, the minutes of the meeting should clearly show that the results of the review contain decisions and actions pertaining to the following:

Outputs
■ Improvement of the effectiveness of the quality management system and its processes
■ Improvement of product related to customer requirements
■ Allocation of the resources needed

TIPS FOR CONDUCTING THE REVIEW

Organizations often struggle to carry out the management review process effectively. This becomes evident in the lack of content in the meeting minutes. Review meetings should be conducted using an agenda and good meeting skills. For example, a formalized format that contains the required inputs and outputs of management review allows for better note taking and ensures that required topics are not left out.

Remember that the minutes of the meetings are a valuable record of the system. Good note taking is a talent. Too often, poor note taking leads to incomplete minutes, which leads to poor follow-up and few improvements. Make sure that the person taking notes understands his or her role, which includes accurate recording of the information, clarifying with the team if questions arise, and recording due dates and persons assigned to tasks. The team also has a responsibility to review what has been written in order to make corrections. Because it's difficult for one person to listen, take notes, and successfully facilitate the meeting, it's recommended that management consider recruiting someone in the company to record the minutes.

FREQUENCY OF REVIEWS

To meet the requirements of the 1994 standards, many organizations held management review meetings only once a year. Unfortunately, trends in data from certain indicators may require a more frequent review.

Holding yearly review meetings may allow management to meet the standard's requirements, but it doesn't truly demonstrate that management is using the information from their quality management system to manage the business. More successful approaches may include:

■ Quarterly reviews covering all aspects of the system
■ Quarterly reviews covering 25 percent of the required review topics (A full year of meetings covers 100 percent of the system review)
■ Monthly reviews that cover a key aspect of the system such that the entire system is reviewed during a year's period of time
■ Incorporating the review topics into regular management meetings

Managers who think of ISO 9001:2000 as a management tool are far ahead of those who are merely going through the motions of maintaining compliance by conducting a meeting. Incorporating the review topics into regular management meetings can be beneficial in using the information from the system to provide insights into changes the business may need to make. This can happen weekly, monthly, or quarterly. The important thing to do is to define when the required topics will be covered and then be concise in capturing minutes, including the decisions and the actions to be taken. Another important component of the management review is to adequately assign ownership for action items with a required due date for completion to ensure follow through and verification of actions. If no one takes responsibility for an action item, it simply won't happen.

MAKING MANAGEMENT REVIEWS MEANINGFUL
People attending management review meetings are often unsure of what they should be looking at or discussing in the meetings in order to ensure the continuing suitability, adequacy, and effectiveness of the quality management system. Also, sometimes it doesn't seem as if there is any correlation between the review topics and what is actually happening in the organization. So, how does management conduct a meaningful, successful management review?

First, identify what should be analyzed and who is responsible for compiling the information and when. Don't place the burden of the information gathering on the management representative. Gathering of information should be spread out to other managers who are responsible for the areas where the information is generated. Creating a table that presents the type of information collected, frequency, and responsibility is helpful in defining what will be presented for management review. This table may also be helpful in meeting the requirements under ISO 9001:2000's Section 8 Measurement, analysis, and improvement. (See Table 4.1 in Chapter 4, Management Representative.)

Second, it's important that the information brought to the meeting be presented in such a way that trends are identifiable. This means that raw data or spreadsheets should be converted into representative pictures. Graphs and charts can work wonders in communicating the data. Information compiled and compared using percentages are also beneficial. While this may sound simple, there are many organizations that shoot from the hip when presenting their results and try to decipher the raw data during the meeting.

Third, identify what the organization should look for when reviewing the required topics and what actions should be taken if trends are positive or negative. Examples of questions that may be considered include: What do results of audits mean to the organization? Have customer and third-party audit results been included in the analysis? What story does the information tell?

QUESTIONS FOR MANAGEMENT REVIEW

Management should consider the following questions when covering the various input and output topics. Keep in mind that the intent of the management review meeting is to review information, ask questions, and assign actions. It's not to be used as a forum for specifically solving each problem.

AUDIT RESULTS

Management sometimes struggles when reviewing information from the audit results as to what should be discussed. Some questions that may facilitate this discussion include:

■ When auditing a particular requirement, are the same problems being recorded? For example, when auditing preventive maintenance, is the maintenance not being performed according to the procedure? When auditing corrective action, do repeat problems continue to be identified? Are there perpetual glitches in the design department where design meetings are not held or the designated people don't attend? Recurring issues should be a red flag for management to take action. This can be done through the corrective and preventive action system.

Another line of questioning should include whether the audits are taking place according to the schedule and if the audit system is supported.

■ Does management cancel audits?

■ Do departments cooperate with the auditors and the audit schedule?

■ Does management respond to their corrective actions in a timely fashion?
■ Does management support the audit system by participating in opening and closing meetings?
■ Are their enough auditors available to conduct the audits?

Audit results are typically seen over a longer period of time because many requirements may not be audited more than once during a year. It's important to compare audits year to year to identify trends. Also, include the trends from your third-party and customer audit results. Compare these to the internal audit results and look for similar trends.

CUSTOMER FEEDBACK

Customer feedback used for management review should link to the process for gathering customer data in Section 8 of the standard. This information should be a combination of both satisfaction and dissatisfaction feedback. It's important to compare the information over time to identify trends. For example, if you are conducting customer surveys, have you seen a shift in the customer's perception since the last survey? How does this compare to the number and type of complaints you are receiving? Other questions may include:
■ What type of complaints do customers have about your products or services?
■ What is the frequency of the complaints?
■ Do the complaints occur with certain customers or certain products?
■ What is the monetary significance of the complaints?
■ Do you proactively solicit information from customers on their future needs?

When addressing customer complaints, questions linking customer data to the corrective and preventive action system should also be considered. For instance, should the complaint be moved into the corrective action loop, or is it a one-time occurrence that should simply be watched? How is complaint data collected? What is the cost to the organization when errors occur and the organization fixes the problem? Are the customers that buy the most also the most profitable?

Many other questions may be prompted by the actual data collected. If the customer data is lacking, don't fall prey to the excuse that your organization doesn't have feedback. There's a good chance that feedback, such as complaints, is not being recorded and is being handled on the fly. Management should know who collects the data and the method used for making decisions about customer information and feedback systems. Assigning the wrong personnel to collect customer information will result in a missed opportunity for improvements.

PROCESS PERFORMANCE

Process issues are not as frequently identified, especially if the organization is more focused on product measurements. Process performance relates to process control, which includes all the processes upstream, i.e., purchasing and contract review. Questions that should be considered include:

■ How many problems identified (either through audits, nonconforming reports, customer complaints, or corrective actions) can be attributed to process problems?

■ Currently, what measures show that the processes in place to produce products and services meet the customers' needs?

■ Have processes been adequately defined and do they operate the majority of the time without error?

■ Are the processes adequately linked together or are gaps apparent between processes and departments? Example, suppliers' nonconformances may be identified in receiving or the production departments, but no mechanism is in place to communicate this information to purchasing.

Some measures that might be considered to identify process issues include accuracy of orders, on-time delivery, cycle time, cost reduction, and efficiency reports. It may be necessary to compare this data month-to-month, quarter-to-quarter, and year-to-year to establish trends.

PRODUCT CONFORMANCE

Determining whether product conforms to requirements can be accomplished by using nonconforming reports, customer feedback, and supplier nonconformances. Product measurements through statistical techniques can also be used to yield product conformance information. Questions that should be asked include:

■ Do the nonconforming reports show that there are more problems with one component than others?

■ Is the information from customer complaints relating to product problems being used to make changes to the product? For example, customer complaints may be recorded but the information not be communicated to the design department in order to address the changes.

■ What types of problems have been identified with the materials that suppliers are providing?

■ What measures have been established to monitor and measure product characteristics and demonstrate that the product meets requirements? What story does this information tell?

■ How many product measures are taken? What actions are implemented based on the results?

STATUS OF CORRECTIVE AND PREVENTIVE ACTIONS

Management should consider the efficiency and effectiveness of their corrective/preventive action system. Questions that should be asked include: How many corrective/preventive actions have been initiated for the year? What other processes or systems have the actions come from (i.e., audits, management review, nonconforming reports, and customer feedback)? How many preventive actions have been initiated for potential problems? How many corrective/preventive actions are still open? What actions continue to repeat themselves, implying that the action taken was not effective? These questions are important for the following reasons:

■ If actions are only generated from audits, the system is not fully functioning to capture important process and product issues that may exist.

■ If no preventive actions are being initiated, it could mean that the trends are not being analyzed to eliminate potential problems and the organization is only working on after-the-fact issues.

■ If actions or less complex issues are still open after six months or a year, it is possible that issues are not being solved effectively and efficiently.

Although some problems may take longer to resolve, open corrective/preventive actions could mean that resources aren't available, the personnel assigned to the problem don't know how to resolve it, or the problem has been incorrectly assigned. Also, open actions could be the result of the problem's root cause not being identified, of too many problems being dumped into the system without a method for prioritizing them, or of a lack of commitment to resolving the issue. In order to determine if the corrective/preventive action process is operating effectively, management should watch for an overabundance of missed completion dates or for constant requests for extensions to due dates.

FOLLOW-UP ACTIONS FROM EARLIER MANAGEMENT REVIEWS

An efficient method for collecting management review minutes is often lacking in many organizations. One of the most frequent findings during audits is the lack of follow-through on an action from the time of assignment through completion. Management review minutes, as stated previously, should be collected so that items such as follow-up actions can be effectively monitored. The minutes should be meaty enough that they describe the results of the actions taken. If actions are postponed or changed, the minutes should explain what will happen and why as a result of the change. Questions that should be asked include:

■ Have the actions from the previous review meetings been addressed?
■ Have the actions been completed or do they need to be reissued?
■ Do the minutes adequately describe the status of the actions?

CHANGES THAT COULD AFFECT THE QUALITY MANAGEMENT SYSTEM

Lack of communication about changes that will be made to equipment, computer systems, layoffs, and changes in key personnel can have a devastating effect on the quality management system. Although some of these things are kept under wraps for very good business reasons, not discussing them with key managers, including the management representative might cause future noncompliances and customer problems. Keep in mind that changes, such as those listed above, can affect processes, procedures, and responsibilities, which make up a well-linked quality management system. Planning for these changes should include identification of the impact that the changes will have on the overall system, revision of procedures and training to the changes, and determination of the resources needed. Management should also review the policy and objectives to determine if modifications will be needed.

Some questions that management should consider are: What external/internal business factors might affect the system? Business factors may include acquisitions, mergers, new product introductions, new customers, and building expansions. Once these factors are identified, what actions need to be put in place to ensure that the quality management system's processes continue to be linked and function efficiently? Effective planning and communication of these changes must be handled in a timely fashion in order to prevent system break down. The management representative should also be included in the discussions in order to ensure that any changes are effectively implemented.

RECOMMENDATIONS FOR IMPROVEMENT AND RESOURCES

Before management completes their review, they must ensure that recommendations for improvements are addressed. This can be done after each input topic is reviewed or at the end of the meeting, taking into account all of the information presented. Improvements could also be recommended at the end of the year, during which all trended information would be presented and incorporated into the planning process. At a minimum, the recommendations for improvement should be determined from the effectiveness of the quality management system and its processes as well as improvements of the product as it relates to customer requirements. Furthermore, these improvements should directly relate to the defined quality objectives. Questions that management may consider include:

■ What improvements need to be made based on the analysis of the data?

■ How do the recommendations for improvement help to achieve the quality objectives?

■ Do the policy and objectives need to be redefined to obtain the improvements or changes needed?

■ What is the time frame for implementation of the improvements?

■ What resources will be needed to implement the improvements?

When planning improvements, the timing of implementation and other planned activities should be considered. For example, if errors are consistently being made at order entry, then overhauling the order entry process to reduce the number of errors wouldn't be justified if the organization is planning to computerize the system. A short-term improvement may be to redefine the manual system and incorporate extra checkpoints to ensure fewer errors until the new system is up and running. Resources would need to be identified for both the short-term fix and the long-term goal. Both recommendations would result in improvement and require resources to modify processes in the quality management system.

It's important to note that management doesn't need to make recommendations for improvement and then solve the problem. Rather, they must be able to communicate the bigger picture of the organization's present and future activities that will assist all those involved, thus making more prudent decisions when determining the solutions. They must also ensure that the recommendations for improvement include decisions about resources.

IN A NUTSHELL

Incorporating management reviews into the day-to-day business of an organization makes sense because this information can give incredible insight into the organization for improvement activities. When organizations begin to integrate the performance of their quality management system with their marketing efforts, objectives, and financial performance, they will discover that ISO 9001:2000's requirements are an important tool, not just a stack of procedures.

Top management should determine how to effectively utilize the management review process within the organization. After several successful management review cycles, top management will gain a clear understanding of the purpose of these meetings as well as maintain the commitment to keep them going, thus paving the path for continual improvement.

Management Review
In a Nutshell...

● Top management must periodically evaluate the suitability, adequacy, and the effectiveness of the quality management system.

● The health of the quality management system can be determined by assessing opportunities for improvement and the need for changes to the quality management system, including the quality policy and quality objectives.

● Taking good notes in management review meetings is essential to demonstrate the depth of management's involvement in the review process.

"Managers who think of ISO 9001:2000 as a management tool are far ahead of those who are merely going through the motions of maintaining compliance by conducting a meeting."

Chapter 7

Utilizing Customer Feedback

Many organizations struggle with the fundamental step of identifying customers and their requirements. Without making this basic determination, organizations are unable to deliver a product and/or service that will be of value to their customers, resulting in inventory that takes up valuable space collecting dust because someone was guessing what customers wanted.

Unlike the 1994 version, ISO 9001:2000 includes new requirements that are specifically focused on the organization's customers. This concept is illustrated in the process model diagram contained in ISO 9001:2000 that links the customer requirements to products or services, measurement of customer satisfaction, and management's responsibility to ensure that customer requirements are determined and met.

The following provides a brief description of each section within ISO 9001:2000 that focuses on the "voice of the customer."

CUSTOMER FOCUS

This section states that top management must ensure that determining and meeting the customer's requirements accomplishes the end result of enhancing customer satisfaction. Although this section is short, it has a powerful message: Know what your customers want, deliver it, and satisfy them.

Many organizations have developed pieces of this process, however, very few have the complete process effectively implemented. To meet this requirement, top management should consider what processes are already in place to identify customer requirements. After this investigation, the next step is determining how this information is communicated to those responsible for converting these requirements into a product or service. This second step is the "product realization process." Converting these requirements is often associated with the creation of job tickets, work orders, quality plans, and so on. The final step is to ascertain if a customer feedback system is in place that captures the necessary information on what customers think about the product and/or service the organization has provided. The customers' feedback, both good and bad, plays an integral part in the management review process because management can utilize this information to effectively make decisions on improvement opportunities. This feedback may be received through complaint systems, customer surveys, comment cards, customer visits, and the like.

7.2 CUSTOMER-RELATED PROCESSES

This section is broken up into three subsections. Two of the three sections are new requirements. Each section deals with a different aspect of customer interaction.

7.2.1 DETERMINATION OF REQUIREMENTS RELATED TO THE PRODUCT

This section focuses specifically on the type of customer requirements that must be determined:

■ Customer-specific product requirements, including delivery and post-delivery requirements

■ Requirements not stated by the customer but necessary for specified use or known and intended use

■ Regulatory and statutory requirements related to product

■ Additional requirements determined by the organization

Top management should ensure that an effectively implemented process exists for determining these types of requirements. Many production problems stem from inadequate information gathered on the front end. This problem can be at least partially remedied if personnel who are often responsible for interacting with the customers, such as sales and customer service, are clearly aware of the organization's requirements for collecting information. Furthermore, how this information is converted, changed, and communicated becomes equally important. Management should ensure that the systems they have in place for transferring the information from processes such as order entry through manufacturing can do so with minimal error.

7.2.2 REVIEW OF REQUIREMENTS RELATED TO THE PRODUCT

These requirements are basically the same as ISO 9001:1994's 4.3 Contract Review clause. Organizations must understand their customers' requirements and have the ability to meet the requirements *prior* to accepting any orders. Any issues with the contract must be resolved before it is processed. If there is a change to the contract after it has been accepted, the appropriate personnel must be notified.

Top management should ensure that the contract review process has been implemented effectively and is functioning efficiently. It's a good idea to reevaluate the process and determine if improvements can be made. The key point to remember is that the organization is absolutely clear on what the customer requirements are before it begins the product-realization process.

7.2.3 CUSTOMER COMMUNICATION

Organizations are now required to determine and implement effective "arrangements" (methods) for communicating with their customers. Many organizations do this, but may not have their process formalized. The information between the organization and its customers is related to products, inquiries, contracts, order handling, changes, complaints, and feedback.

Although many organizations have customer service departments that handle customer interactions, some organizations have these duties handled by various departments. Regardless of the structure, it's imperative for top management to confirm that an effective and efficient communication channel is established so customers can conveniently communicate feedback. Some organizations have established "customer engineers" who have specific responsibilities for most of the customer communication and interaction. These personnel deal with customer satisfaction/dissatisfaction issues, product/service quality issues, site visits, and other issues.

8.2.1 CUSTOMER SATISFACTION

This requirement states that organizations must monitor customer perceptions as one of the performance measurements of their quality management system and must determine the methodologies for obtaining and using this information. For many organizations, this requirement may be simple to meet, but for others it may be a challenge. The level of difficulty depends on the maturity of the organization and its relationship with its customers. It also depends on whether an organization currently has an effective customer satisfaction measurement system.

MONITORING AND MEASURING CUSTOMER SATISFACTION

Organizations will need to candidly ask themselves if they know whether their own perception of how they satisfy the customer matches what the customer really thinks. Understanding this information is necessary before an organization can determine what it must do to create an effective system for monitoring and measuring customer perceptions.

UNDERSTANDING THE CUSTOMER

Customer needs are driven by problems that the customer is trying to solve. These needs will exist until the customer has found the product or service to fill the need. However, customer satisfaction is more than just meeting a customer need. Many times, customers don't really know what they need, but they can often explain the expectation they have about the product or service. These expectations are formed through the customer's previous experiences and by suppliers' descriptions of their products and services.

Both needs and expectations come into play when determining how to monitor customer satisfaction. For example, if a customer is purchasing components for circuit boards, the "need" is components. However, the customer's expectation is to purchase components that achieve a certain defective parts per million (DPM) level and are delivered on time. This expectation has been created by either the performance the supplier has previously demonstrated or by that of other competing suppliers. Even though the need may be met, if expectations are not satisfied, customer perceptions will begin to erode. Understanding the aspect of perceptions is vitally important, as many organizations' reputations are built on the expectations they have created and how consistently they achieve them. Most people are familiar with the exemplary customer service that organizations like Nordstrom and Disney have created. Organizations like these have raised the bar for the consumer to now expect that all department stores or theme parks will treat their customers in the same way. This is why it's important for organizations to know their customers' expectations as well as their needs, because simply producing the product or service might not be enough to retain the customer.

Keep in mind that product specifications can be measured directly. Customer perceptions are indirect or subjective and the methods used to measure them will be different than those used to measure the product.

COLLECTING CUSTOMER INFORMATION

Most organizations have established some method of collecting customer information through their complaint system. Unfortunately, many haven't given much consideration to who will collect the complaints, the method of collection, or the criteria that will instigate actions when complaints are received. Complaint systems often give way to crisis management, and this is where they stop. The complaint system should be used as a means by which the customer can convey issues or problems. It should spur people into action, and it should cause thought-provoking questions *after* the crisis has been solved.

One common flaw of complaint systems is the method by which information comes into the company from the customer. Often, only the sales or customer service employees are gathering the customer feedback. When this happens, the information might be biased when problems that don't shed a negative light on the individual or department are the only ones to be recorded. This isn't to suggest that these departments shouldn't collect the data. However, top management should clearly communicate that the collection of customer complaint information is critical and should investigate if no complaint information is reported, especially if scrap rates and nonconforming material reports are plentiful.

Because the review of customer feedback is required during management review, the method of collecting information should be clearly defined. When a complaint is received, the most important action is to take care of the customer and resolve the issue right then, if possible. This is considered the interim action. Next, someone would review the issue to determine if the problem should go into the corrective action system. Not every issue will become a corrective action. The ones that do enter the system will require a formal root-cause analysis investigation before adequate corrective action can be determined.

Management should decide upon the criteria for moving a customer complaint into the corrective action system. This could be based on issues such as a dollar amount, the type of problem, the frequency of the problem, and the customer involved. If the complaints don't require corrective action, they should be collected, sorted, and analyzed for management review. During this review, management can analyze any trends that could be addressed through preventive actions. Remember that complaints are records of after-the-fact problems and are not indicators of what the customer thinks about the organization in relationship to competitors, nor do they establish future customer needs. Also, because complaints measure after-the-fact problems, they require the customer to contact the organization. In many cases, customers don't report problems; they just move their business elsewhere.

Organizations need to broaden their focus from only collecting complaint data in order to determine customer perceptions. In conjunction with complaint reporting, surveys and other market research will provide a more complete picture of the customer's perceptions. If management is truly committed to customer satisfaction and continual improvement, they will want to add other methods of collecting customer information besides complaint reporting. These methods may include customer report cards, surveys (both mail and phone), focus groups, and collecting information related to specific customer attributes, such as service delivery or competitor or market analysis.

Red flags should be raised if the following situations present themselves inside the organization. First, if people are confused about what constitutes a complaint, then it must be made clear that a customer contacting the organization regarding any product or service that doesn't meet their needs or expectations is to be considered a complaint. It's immaterial how much of a discount is given, how quickly the goods are reshipped, or how happy the customer is after the error: The bottom line is that the organization has inconvenienced the customer. In a situation like this, the organization begins to lose credibility and money. Concessions, product reruns, and management's time lost dealing with the problem are costly to the organization but are often overlooked when profits are discussed, despite their negative effect on the bottom line.

Second, if the organization needs full-time people or if management has authorized adding extra people to handle the complaints, they should be asking, "If we are doing such a good job with the customer, why do we need all of these people to handle the problems?" Many times the quality department handles the complaints and their voice is not heard at higher levels. Top management should be asking the frontline employees what kinds of issues they are handling and ensure that these problems are not ignored. A focused effort by top management to resolve customer issues sends an important message to the organization: Customers are the reason we are in business and satisfying them is a top priority.

MEASUREMENTS AND CUSTOMER DATA

Collecting the right customer data requires top management to focus on the key areas that are important to their customers and the growth of the business. These key areas should be considered when establishing measurable objectives and should relate to improvement goals.

For example, if on-time delivery is a key objective, management should be looking into customer expectations, knowledge of competition, and types of problems in relation to on-time delivery. If gaps exist, an analysis should be done to determine where improvements can be made. Several issues, such as order entry errors, the customer providing incorrect or late change information, inaccurate scheduling, production failures, incomplete information from sales to engineering, and specification errors, could cause on-time delivery problems. Although on-time delivery is an important measure, the customer may have other more critical issues with the product or service. By not doing some sort of analysis, the organization runs the risk of measuring the wrong thing, which may not improve customer satisfaction.

Establishing measures is not an easy task and should be carefully thought through so that measuring isn't done simply for the sake of measuring. Furthermore, measurements should be easy to understand, applied to the objectives, and easy to collect. If data is difficult to obtain or analyze, the organization risks losing timely, accurate information to drive improvement.

TIPS FOR ANALYZING CUSTOMER DATA

To analyze customer data, managers should use the following guidelines:

1. Utilize effective software, such as a spreadsheet or graphics program, that can turn feedback into meaningful information.
2. Look for trends, both positive and negative, in the feedback. Develop actions to address these trends. Assign responsibility and due dates to each action.
3. Utilize customer feedback for other planning activities, such as market analysis, preventive actions, product development, and expansions.
4. Communicate key information from the customer data analysis within the organization. This can be done through postings, newsletters, or other means. These communication efforts should also link to top management's requirements for customer focus (5.2), internal communication (5.5.3), and the management representative's responsibility to promote customer requirements (5.5.2).

5. Involve appropriate personnel, including decision makers, in the improvement activities. Focus on the actions that will reap the greatest rewards, for both the organization and the customers.

6. Simplify customer data-collection techniques and summarize information effectively.

NINE COMMON MISTAKES

Organizations tend to make common mistakes when gathering information about the customer. Service organizations are often more in tune with customer expectations than are manufacturing environments. Nevertheless, many organizations don't search for the right information or utilize the information they receive to their advantage. Below are nine common mistakes organizations make when collecting and utilizing customer data.

1. *Developing an ineffective customer survey, comment card, or other reporting mechanism.* Top management should ensure that the right questions are used when developing reporting mechanisms. It's important to consider what results (qualitative vs. quantitative) are expected. Many surveys and comment cards use a little of both. However, both of these instruments need to be structured so that the information is quantifiable, which lessens the margin of error. How questions are worded can also skew the results. It's advisable to get professional assistance in designing the survey, collecting the data, or both. Poorly designed instruments will result in the collection of bad data, which is often worse than not collecting any data at all.

2. *Receiving comment cards, surveys, or other survey mechanisms and not analyzing them for trends.* Don't let these items sit on someone's desk and rot. The purpose of collecting this information is to determine where the customers' perceptions are. Once this is known, effective decision making can take place.

3. *Designing an ineffective and/or poorly structured customer-complaint process.* The customer-complaint process should include the key functions and steps necessary to provide timely information (i.e., interim actions, corrective actions) to the customer in the event of nonconformances. Management should clearly and consistently identify when a complaint should be moved into the corrective action system. They should also stress the importance of resolving problems for good, as well as being proactive in the future through determining preventive actions.

4. *Inadequately communicating positive and negative customer feedback and/or data to appropriate personnel.* Customer feedback must be adequately

communicated to the appropriate personnel to facilitate improvement actions. For example, customer return information should be communicated directly to the design personnel in order to make design changes to the product that will prevent future customer returns. The personnel who actually manufacture the product also need to be notified of customer issues because, typically, they have some of the best improvement ideas. Finally, organizations should look at what management level is receiving the feedback information. For example, if a bank's comment card contains an elaborate customer promise from its president but the card is addressed to the local branch, a customer who has a problem with that branch will believe that there is no method to communicate to a higher level of management.

Communicating positive feedback to personnel within the organization is just as important as communicating the negative feedback. This information can also be trended to help top management determine what they are doing right. Keep in mind that ISO 9001:2000 requires customer feedback to be considered during management review, which should include both positive and negative feedback. Furthermore, positive feedback can be communicated to the organization through items such as newsletters, e-mail, organizational meetings, and posters.

5. *Filtering and not adequately recording customer complaint information.* If the customer-complaint system has few recorded complaints, it could be because the organization provides a superior product or service, or it could be because important customer feedback is not being recorded accurately. Sometimes information is filtered by those who collect the feedback to protect themselves or their department. To prevent this from happening, management should examine nonconforming product reports and audit reports that note process or system issues. Talking to the receiving or quality departments to find out how many customer returns have come through the door may also provide an interesting picture because these customer returns aren't always added to the complaint or nonconforming product reporting system.

6. *Using the customer complaint system as the only method for collecting customer feedback.* In the service industry, frontline employees handle many of the customer complaints. These may never be recorded or reach top management because the system may not be conducive for collecting information, or the negative customer feedback may personally reflect on the employee. Therefore, management must carefully determine if they are receiving a complete picture of customer feedback. If the complaint system is the only method being used, the picture will be incomplete. Furthermore, if the complaint system is the only measure of satisfaction, the

organization may miss valuable feedback from the customer on future needs that could result in a competitive advantage.

7. *Not establishing across the organization what constitutes a customer complaint.* It's imperative that personnel agree on what type of customer feedback is logged as an official customer complaint. Unless this is made clear from the outset, many legitimate complaints may not be recorded, or unnecessary information may jam the complaint system.

8. *Not including customer feedback as an input to management review.* ISO 9001:2000 requires that customer feedback be one of the inputs to the management review process. This feedback information should be summarized in enough detail that effective decision making and improvement recommendations take place.

9. *Incorrectly identifying the areas that are important to the customer before setting up measurements.* Organizations should be clear on their customer requirements, because these are what drive the customer's decision-making choices. Unless organizations are tuned in to these requirements and have correct measurements in place, they will waste time and effort collecting useless data.

IN A NUTSHELL

Top management should ensure that the data generated from the customer satisfaction measures is used as an input for the management review process. This new requirement within ISO 9001:2000 will cause top managers to take a serious look at how well the organization is satisfying its customers. Auditors will confirm if the customer satisfaction process has mechanisms in place to ensure that the customer complaints are investigated for root cause and that actions taken are effective in solving the problem. Furthermore, top management should ensure that the appropriate personnel, especially the decision makers, are involved in the customer satisfaction process.

ISO 9001:2000 incorporates requirements that will benefit the organization and its customers. These requirements are found throughout the standard, implying the distinct linkage of customers with the internal business processes. Understanding this linkage is critical for top management to effectively develop and lead a customer-focused organization. Once an organization truly understands the "voice of its customers," it will be well on its way to becoming a world-class organization.

Utilizing Customer Feedback In a Nutshell...

● Top management must ensure that determining and meeting the customer's requirements accomplishes the end result of enhancing customer satisfaction.

● Customer feedback, both good and bad, plays an integral part in the management review process because management can utilize this information to effectively make decisions on improvement opportunities.

● It's imperative for top management to confirm that an effective and efficient communication channel is established so customers can conveniently communicate feedback.

● Monitoring information relating to customer perceptions is a required measurement of the performance of the quality management system.

"If management is truly committed to customer satisfaction and continual improvement, they will want to add other measures of collecting customer information besides complaint reporting."

Chapter 8

Continual Improvement and Management Responsibility

A new requirement in ISO 9001:2000 states that top management must be committed to continually improving the effectiveness of the quality management system. The standard specifically lists in 8.5.1 Continual improvement what the organization must use to make this happen:

■ Quality policy
■ Quality objectives
■ Audit results
■ Analysis of data
■ Corrective and preventive actions
■ Management review

The standard purposely links top management to the continual improvement process. In fact, some of the items listed in 8.5.1 also appear under the requirements for 5.6 Management review. Understanding this direct linkage will require top management to question how effective the current integration of these items is within their organization.

Continual improvement is more than just fixing a problem; it's a philosophy or mindset that an organization must have in all aspects of its business. For example, customer requirements should be the driving factor when management determines their organizational objectives. This may sound simplistic, but too many organizations aren't knowledgeable about important customer data, which, if used effectively, can drive improvement. Although most know who their top customer is in sales volume, they don't know who their top customer is in terms of profitability. This important link is often missed. High sales volume does not necessarily mean high profitability.

For example, suppose an organization prizes its multimillion-dollar customer. The organization bends over backwards to accommodate this customer's every need and makes concessions or deals with the customer on every request. The organization installs computer systems and special processes to satisfy this customer and bumps smaller customers' orders to ensure the prized customer gets any demanded schedule. When all of this is done, management can't figure out why sales are up but profits are down. So they set higher sales goals to sell more. Unfortunately, while more and more orders are produced, the profit picture plateaus or takes a downward spiral. Jobs are cut to alleviate expenses and improve the bottom line, and the vicious cycle continues.

This example illustrates a typical scenario wherein the organization is caught up in a quick-fix cycle. In this example, top management should step back and assess the current situation to determine what really needs improvement. They are only able to do this effectively if they approach the situation from a different perspective. In doing this, they would ask such questions as: What are the total costs (e.g., computer systems, concessions, bumping smaller orders, and time to manage) associated with keeping this customer? Do the demands of this customer move the organization away from its purpose and objectives? How does the organization define this customer's satisfaction, and how far will it go to attain it? Does the commission structure of the sales force promote quantity of sales vs. quality of sales?

Asking these types of out-of-the-box questions will help top management drive improvement by tying its policy, objectives, and measurements together.

Figure 8.1 illustrates how top management plays an integral part in the continual improvement of the organization. Top management must effectively utilize information from the quality management system to make informed decisions and take action on identified opportunities for improvement.

DEVELOPING A CONTINUAL IMPROVEMENT PROCESS

ISO 9001:2000 has taken into consideration the Plan-Do-Check-Act cycle when developing processes. This cycle should also be applied when evaluating the effectiveness of the quality management system. While this model seems relatively simple, it's implemented in many organizations in word only. This model is often difficult to implement because organizations get caught up in the "doing." Many organizations do very little planning when it comes to improvement activities or root-cause analysis.

Instead, personnel react to problems rather than finding ways to prevent them in the first place.

In order to develop an effective continual improvement process, top management must be actively committed to making it happen. They must ensure that all components of the continual improvement loop shown in Figure 8.1 are effectively implemented within their system. The first step is to determine what components are currently missing and what steps are necessary to close the gaps. Many organizations have underutilized their

Figure 8.1: Continual Improvement Loop

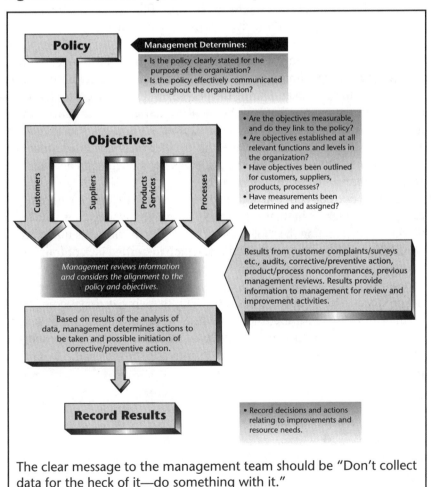

management review process by not identifying deficiencies in the system and taking actions to correct them. Furthermore, follow-up and closure of corrective actions don't take place in order to verify effectiveness of implementation. Without this critical last step, improvements never happen.

To achieve continual improvement of the effectiveness of a quality management system, it's important to understand how processes within the system are linked. The following case study shows one organization's approach to continual improvement.

The Case of the Nonconforming Tubing

The Tubber Tubing Co. established its ISO 9002 system in 1997, and is in the process of upgrading its quality management system to ISO 9001:2000. Tubber manufactures, but does not design, tubing for hospital use. Tubber also produces some of this tubing from customer-supplied plastic. The tubing administers drugs and must be of a certain dimension specified by the customer. During the past several months, customers have complained and returned several shipments because the inner diameter was not manufactured correctly per the customer's tolerance specifications. Management is concerned because the problem has escalated since the last management review. Also, the issue has been documented within the corrective/preventive action system.

Because two corrective actions had been previously issued without success, management is in total support of a thorough investigation. The team works on determining the root cause of the problem and takes into consideration the previous corrective actions, which identified lack of training as a cause. While this is being done, management supports the effort by allocating extra resources for additional inspections to prevent nonconforming product from reaching the customer. This extra inspection is considered an interim action until the true root cause is found. The team did a thorough job of problem solving and reviewed information from many sources to get closer to the root cause. The results are shown on the following pages.

Source Reviewed	Purpose of Review	Result
Calibration Records	To determine if dimension-measuring equipment had been calibrated according to schedule and to reexamine the results of the calibration	Records from the past eight months indicated that the calibrations were done monthly per the schedule with positive results. However, a piece of equipment was reported missing for the past eight months and therefore had been replaced with a new technology.
Training Records	To determine if those who measure the product had received identified training and whether the training had been evaluated for effectiveness	Training had been performed according to the needs identified. However, the effectiveness of the training that took place six months ago could not be verified.
Internal Audit Records	To determine if previous audit records had indicated deviation from production practices that might affect conformance of product	Audits indicated that the missing measurement equipment still appeared on the calibration records with no calibrations recorded.
Noncon-forming Reports	To determine if nonconforming reports had identified the tubing problem during production processes	Nonconforming reports had been filed 16 times in the last eight months for problems with tubing dimension. The bulk of the problems identified were on second shift.

Source Reviewed	Purpose of Review	Result
SPC Charts	To determine if deviations had occurred, their frequency, and on which shift	SPC charts showed variances outside of the tolerance ranges during manufacturing runs a total of 24 times within the last eight months and occurred on the second shift.
Customer Complaints	To determine how many customer complaints surrounding the tubing issue identified the same problem	Twenty-four customer complaints indicated reports of the tubing dimension increasing (in the last eight months).
Customer Job Specification Sheets	To determine if customer requirements and company requirements had been adequately recorded	Upon review of the customer specification sheets, all requirements were accurately recorded.
Receiving Reports	To determine if customer-supplied property received had been flagged due to damage or unsuitability	Receiving reports indicated that twice within the eight months, customer property had arrived damaged. Customer was contacted and the issue was resolved.

This analysis helped the team to narrow the issues and focus on the following hypotheses:

1. Training might be a concern since the new technology had been introduced and the effectiveness of the training had not been verified. It's possible that the methods for proper use of the new equipment were not being followed.

2. The missing piece of calibration equipment had never been found, although it could possibly still be in use.

3. In the last eight months, nonconforming reports had been issued 16 times for tubing problems and SPC charts showed variances occurring 24 times. This indicates that the problem was being identified during production runs but was uncorrected before being shipped to the customer. Upon reviewing the customer complaints, the products identified on the nonconforming reports were the same ones for which customers had filed complaints. Therefore, the information was available but was not being used. The team further concluded that those authorized to make decisions on correcting the problem might not be reviewing the reports.

4. Because the review of customer job specifications and receiving reports indicated positive results, the team ruled out missing information on customer specification sheets or unsuitable customer-supplied property as probable causes.

With all of this information in hand, the team decided to perform some investigation. To test the first hypothesis, they decided to audit the new equipment's calibration process. They discovered that when operators were asked to demonstrate how the equipment was used, they gave inconsistent answers. The team found a handwritten step-by-step users' guide taped to the bench, with no evidence of document control. They also discovered that second-shift personnel utilized the missing piece of measurement equipment to keep up with schedule demands and production needs. In fact, this out-of-calibration piece of equipment was not missing; it was stored in a production cabinet awaiting use.

The team then investigated why no one had identified an issue with these products, even though nonconforming reports had indicated problems. Upon the review of the data analysis process, the team found that management reviewed information on product conformance during quarterly management review meetings. Because production supervisors and managers submitted this information quarterly, they didn't review or use it within their own departments on a monthly basis. Furthermore, the team found that, although objectives and plans for satisfying customers were outlined, the plans were not specific in detailing who would be responsible for analyzing or using the information within the quality management system other than during management reviews.

After completing a thorough investigation, the team recommended to management that the following actions be taken:

■ The step-by-step calibration guideline for operators should be reviewed for accuracy, placed under document control, and posted for ease of use.

■ Operators should be retrained on the use of the new measurement equipment, and the effectiveness of this training should be verified through employee testing.

■ The missing piece of calibration equipment should be recalibrated, or a new piece purchased, to ensure that adequate equipment is available during production.

■ Management should specify how information obtained from data analysis should be used to achieve the organization's objectives. This will ensure that information is acted upon prior to quarterly management review meetings.

This case study indicates how the entire system needs to be considered when problem-solving activities get underway with the goal of improvement. The previous example only covers part of the Plan-Do-Check-Act process, and implementation and follow-up steps are needed to effectively complete this cycle to ensure that the solutions that are implemented effectively correct the problem.

IN A NUTSHELL

Continual improvement doesn't happen overnight. A committed effort on the part of management and those closest to the work needs to exist for improvements to be made. This means that data gathering is useless unless the right people can effectively utilize the information in a timely manner to institute change.

As in the case of the Tubber Tubing Co. example, many organizations generate SPC charts and other measurements only to file them away until a crisis occurs. Data is irrelevant if it doesn't link to a goal or objective. Organizations should look at the number of reports, the relevance of the reports, how the data is tied to objectives and goals, and who is responsible to analyze the information. Furthermore, someone must be able to answer the "if" questions: If the information indicates negative numbers, what actions should be taken? If the information indicates positive trends, then what? Keep in mind that collecting positive data is just as important as collecting negative data even though it's often overlooked in the attempt to fix problems. Positive data can provide the organization with insights about its strengths, competitive advantages, and employee satisfaction.

Finally, setting meaningful measures for objectives is necessary if continual improvement is to take place. However, measurements are sometimes treated as though they're insignificant, as in the 1980s when many organizations' walls were plastered with charts and graphs meant to propel them to immediate success. Measurements alone will not guarantee success, and many measures aren't always relevant to the goals of the organization. In the 1980s, departments were told to establish measurements without being educated on the organization's objectives and the link between the measures and these goals. Additionally, many elaborate schemes were designed for developing and capturing this type of information, but no follow-through occurred during the development of specific actions to drive improvement efforts. Effective continual improvement activities start with management and end with management. Management needs to ensure that measurable objectives are established and that the review of these goals and follow-through occurs.

Achieving continual improvement will always be a challenge. However, one thing is certain: When management plays an active role in guiding the continual improvement process, success is sure to follow.

Continual Improvement and Management Responsibility In a Nutshell...

● The standard purposely links top management to the continual improvement process.

● Continual improvement is more than just fixing a problem; it's a philosophy or mindset that an organization must have in all aspects of its business.

● To achieve continual improvement of the effectiveness of a quality management system, it's important to understand how processes within the system are linked.

"Top management must effectively utilize information from the quality management system to make informed decisions and take action on identified opportunities for improvement."

Chapter 9

Frequently Asked Questions for Management

1. What happens if the executive management team in my company isn't interested in participating in the quality management system?

Because ISO 9001:2000 has additional management responsibility requirements, many managers may feel overwhelmed by the changes. However, to become and remain compliant to ISO 9001:2000, the management team will need to participate. If the management team is educated on the new requirements and given ideas for implementation and compliance, they may be more willing to participate. By not participating, management loses the benefit of using ISO 9001 as a tool for improving the organization, plus they run the risk of not achieving or losing their certification.

2. How do I effectively communicate the changes in management responsibility to all of the different sites within my organization?

Refer to the book *ISO 9000:2000 In a Nutshell* to understand all of the specific management responsibility requirements. Once a communication process is defined, e-mail, intranets, the Internet, conference calls, and on-site presentations for transmitting the information can be utilized. Sometimes, information presented to top management by an expert outside of the organization may be more helpful because it allows the management team to ask candid questions and receive guidance. These presentations can also help the management representative convey the requirements.

3. What happens if members of our executive management team are replaced with new personnel?

The new managers will need to be trained in the components of the ISO 9001:2000 standard. They will also need training regarding the organization's quality management system, with particular emphasis on management responsibility, the quality policy, quality objectives, and the continual improvement process. Third-party auditors are always interested in knowing whether changes have occurred in key management positions. Changes of this type should be communicated to your third-party registrar prior to your next audit. Often, when these changes occur, some of the management requirements fall out of compliance. Third-party auditors will check management review minutes and planning activities to ensure that new management is successfully carrying out the requirements of the standard.

4. Why isn't the quality policy enough to demonstrate management's commitment?

The quality policy is simply a documented statement. It doesn't demonstrate anything. Management commitment is demonstrated through communication of quality objectives, provision of adequate resources for the quality management system, and participation in management review meetings. In other words, actions speak louder than words.

5. Why did ISO expand the management requirements?

The intent of the ISO 9001:2000 standard is to help organizations focus on process management, customers, and continual improvement. To succeed, management must be committed to the quality management system and must demonstrate this commitment through active participation. ISO 9001:1994 did not make these requirements clear, and, therefore, many managers didn't actively participate in supporting the requirements.

6. Does our organization have to develop a new quality policy?

No. It's suggested that you review the quality policy to ensure that it encompasses all of the elements important to your organization as it relates to the quality of your organization's products and/or services. It should also be aligned with the quality objectives. ISO 9001:2000 requires that the objectives be measurable and consistent with the policy. Third-party auditors may ask management how the objectives and policy are related and how this information is communicated within the organization. Also, the standard requires that the policy and objectives be evaluated for changes during management review.

7. What happens if the results of our improvement activities don't show positive trends?

It will be necessary to demonstrate that you have all of the components of a continual improvement system in place, such as management review, corrective/preventive action, and internal audits. It's essential to demonstrate to your third-party auditor that actions are being taken through these systems to address any adverse trends. Also, it's important to show how your organization analyzes data in an effort to identify opportunities for improvement.

8. At a minimum, who in our organization should understand the eight quality management principles?

The executive management team, middle managers, the ISO coordinator, management representatives, and internal auditors should all be familiar with the intent of the principles. Because the principles are solid philosophies for managing an organization, it's suggested that they be integrated into the quality policy and objectives and communicated throughout the organization.

9. With the new management review requirements, should we schedule our reviews more frequently?

That is entirely up to your management team. However, it's recommended that management reviews of the quality management system be conducted at least twice a year. Many organizations meet monthly or quarterly and review portions of the system at each meeting. Also, some organizations incorporate their reviews with other management meetings and achieve positive results. Keeping informed of the issues on a frequent basis will benefit the entire organization and allow for timely actions to be taken.

10. How involved will our marketing and customer service departments need to be in order to meet the new customer-related requirements?

It depends on what customer-related role they play within your organization. If the marketing department is responsible for the determination of customer requirements, then they would need to ensure that those requirements are effectively defined and communicated to appropriate personnel so that the requirements can be adequately converted into a product and/or service. Typically, customer service departments are responsible for handling customer feedback, both positive and negative. If they are responsible for ensuring that customer satisfaction is measured and analyzed, then they would need to understand the new requirements.

11. Do we need to send our customers a customer satisfaction survey to determine their level of satisfaction?

It depends. If a survey is the only mechanism you have available to gather customer information, then it would be appropriate. If, on the other hand, your organization measures and analyzes customer feedback in a different way, then a survey may not be necessary. Either way, it's up to the organization to determine the best method of collecting, analyzing, and utilizing customer satisfaction information. Keep in mind that organizations registered to the 1994 standard have already established one method of collecting customer satisfaction (dissatisfaction) information through the use of their customer complaint system.

12. Will there be additional costs associated with becoming compliant to ISO 9001:2000?

There may be some additional costs, such as training. Several factors will determine the costs, such as top management commitment, the existence of a solid continual improvement process, and the size and complexity of the organization. The extra effort that needs to be put in place to develop and implement any additional requirements will be more costly as will waiting until the end of the three-year transition period to cram the changes into the system.

13. Will our organization be more efficient after we've become compliant to ISO 9001:2000?

Not necessarily. The new standard focuses on improving the effectiveness of the quality management system. To improve the organization's efficiency, it's recommended that ISO 9004:2000, which exceeds the basic requirements of the standard, be used in conjunction with ISO 9001:2000. Keep in mind that ISO 9001 alone won't produce all the results management may want. ISO 9001 is just part of the equation. Other facets of the business, such as motivation of people and sound marketing and financial practices, in conjunction with ISO 9001:2000 registration will produce results.

14. What are some of the ways that top management can demonstrate their commitment to the quality management system?

Top management's commitment is vital to the success of the management system, and this commitment must be constantly and consistently demonstrated. Top management can do this by communicating relevant information about the system; participating in important meetings, such as management review and planning; assigning adequate resources for activities, such as training and internal audits; and allowing personnel adequate time to solve problems.

15. What will third-party auditors look for as evidence of compliance to the new requirements for management responsibility?

Third-party auditors will look for evidence that top management is committed to the quality management system and its effectiveness. They will examine management review minutes to determine how the system is evaluated. They will look for evidence that action plans have been developed and implemented on problem areas. They will also look for evidence that the organization's management review, corrective/preventive action, and internal audit systems are linked and that the system emphasizes continual improvement. If adverse trends exist from the organization's data analysis, auditors will look for actions to address those trends. Furthermore, they will look for established quality objectives and their alignment with the quality policy.

16. What if our organization is not successful in making the transition to ISO 9001:2000 before the transition period has ended?

Making the transition to the new standard will most likely occur over several surveillance audits. Registrars are confident that organizations will be successful in their transition. Contact your registrar for specific details. Of course, if an organization doesn't show a desire to improve its status, the 1994 certificate will lapse and the upgrade process will be discontinued.

17. Now that ISO has discontinued ISO 9002 and ISO 9003, how will organizations registered to these standards differentiate themselves from ISO 9001 companies?

The scope of activities for which the organization has been registered will appear on the certificate. It will be important to accurately communicate this scope of activities to the registrar to ensure that the end customer understands what is included or not included, so they are not misled.

18. Will our internal auditors require more training for ISO 9001:2000?

Yes. Internal auditors will need to be trained on the structure, content, and terminology of the revised standard. The auditors will need to understand the process management concept and will need to develop modified auditing checklists that cover the new requirements. Management should ensure this training is provided by a qualified source.

19. How best should our management team utilize ISO 9004:2000?

ISO 9004:2000 Quality management systems–Guidelines for performance improvements has been designed to be used as part of a consistent pair with ISO 9001:2000. However, these standards can also be used independently. ISO 9004:2000 contains a self-assessment tool to assist organizations in determining the maturity of their quality management system. By using these standards together, organizations can move beyond the minimum requirements of ISO 9001:2000 and focus on the next level of excellence.

20. Where can I find additional information?

There are a number of sources from which to get information:

■ American Society for Quality (ASQ)—(800) 248-1946 or *www.asq.org*
■ Registrar Accreditation Board (RAB)—(888) 722-2440 or *www.rabnet.com*
■ U.S. Standards Group—*standardsgroup.asq.org*
■ International Organization for Standardization (ISO)—*www.iso.ch*
■ ISO TC 176/SC2 Web site—*www.bsi.org.uk/iso-tc176-sc2*

You may also contact the authors of this book:

Jeanne Ketola, CEO
Pathway Consulting Inc.
Minneapolis, Minnesota
www.pathwayconsultinginc.com

Kathy Roberts, President
Sunrise Consulting Inc.
Raleigh, North Carolina
http://thesunrise.home.mindspring.com

Or visit the authors' joint Web site: *www.inanutshellproductions.com*

About the Authors

Jeanne Ketola, CEO of Pathway Consulting Inc., has more than 20 years of business experience in a diverse range of industries. She has a bachelor's degree in business management and is an ASQ Certified Quality Auditor, an RAB Quality Systems Auditor, and a trained management coach. Ketola is actively involved in the U.S. TAG to TC 176, which reviews and approves the ISO 9000 standards for the United States. She has participated at a national level in writing the auditing guidelines for ISO 9000-Q10011. Ketola is the secretary of the ANSI Z1 Executive Committee, which is responsible for all actions relating to national quality standards.

Jeanne Ketola, CEO
Pathway Consulting Inc.
Minneapolis, Minnesota
www.pathwayconsultinginc.com

Kathy Roberts, President of Sunrise Consulting Inc., has held various quality engineering and quality management positions in a diverse range of industries during the past 10 years. She has a bachelor's degree in industrial engineering and is an ASQ Certified Quality Auditor and a trained examiner for the North Carolina Performance Excellence Process. Roberts is an active member of the U.S. TAG to TC 176 and is the vice chair of the ANSI Z1 Executive Committee.

Kathy Roberts, President
Sunrise Consulting Inc.
Raleigh, North Carolina
http://thesunrise.home.mindspring.com

Also visit their joint Web site:
www.inanutshellproductions.com

Index